Y0-CAS-106

Set design by James Kronzer *Photo by James Leynse*

A scene from the New York production of *Opus.*

OPUS

BY MICHAEL HOLLINGER

DRAMATISTS
PLAY SERVICE
INC.

SPECIAL NOTE

Anyone receiving permission to produce OPUS is required to give credit to the Author as sole and exclusive Author of the Play on the title page of all programs distributed in connection with performances of the Play and in all instances in which the title of the Play appears for purposes of advertising, publicizing or otherwise exploiting the Play and/or a production thereof. The name of the Author must appear on a separate line, in which no other name appears, immediately beneath the title and in size of type equal to 50% of the size of the largest, most prominent letter used for the title of the Play. No person, firm or entity may receive credit larger or more prominent than that accorded the Author. The following acknowledgments must appear on the title page in all programs distributed in connection with performances of the Play:

New York premiere produced by Primary Stages in New York City, July 2007
(Casey Childs, Founder and Executive Producer;
Andrew Leynse, Artistic Director; Elliot Fox, Managing Director).

Originally produced by the Arden Theatre Company,
Terrence J. Nolen, Producing Artistic Director, Amy Murphy, Managing Director,
in Philadelphia, PA and City Theatre Company,
Tracy Bridgen, Artistic Director, Greg Quinlan, Managing Director,
in Pittsburgh, PA. The coproduction opened in Philadelphia,
January 2006 and in Pittsburgh, March 2006.

Music courtesy of The Vertigo String Quartet and Arden Theatre Company.

SPECIAL NOTE ON MUSIC

A CD containing music and sheet music is required for production. The cost is $35.00, plus shipping and handling. The nonprofessional fee for the use of this music is $25.00 per performance.

For Stefan — good cellist, great friend

and

In memory of Bob Clay (who introduced me to string quartets),
David Coren (who fostered my love of them),
and Harry Kownatski (who brought me back into the fold)

ACKNOWLEDGMENTS

Thanks to John Steber and the cast of the first-draft reading at New Dramatists; to Tracy Brigden, Kellee Van Aken, Carlyn Aquiline and the cast of the City Theatre reading; to John Wooten and the casts of the Premiere Stages readings; to John Pietrowski, Peter Hays, Jim Glossman and the cast of the Playwrights' Theatre of New Jersey reading; and to Elizabeth Dowd and the cast of the Bloomsburg Theatre Ensemble reading.

I am grateful to Pennsylvania Council on the Arts, which helped subsidize the writing of OPUS, and to Frederick W. Anton, III, for his generous support. Thanks to Drury Stitch, George Ainsley, Emilio Gravagno, Steve Smith, and Stefan Koch for their expertise, and to Harold Coopersmith, Bill Phillips, and Arvid Bloom. Thanks also to Al Hirsig, Bob Fitzpatrick, and Curtis Institute of Music; to Kris Parsons, Bob Capanna, and Settlement Music School; and to the wonderful Vertigo String Quartet. And thanks to Mary Harden and Harden-Curtis Associates, Stephanie Klapper and Associates, and early readers of the play: Megan Bellwoar, Aaron Posner, Harriet Power, Jim Christy, Joanna Rotte, and Phil Setzer.

In addition to the City Theatre staff already mentioned above, I owe much to Amy Dugas Brown, Murph Henderson, and Arden Theatre Company for their labors on the splendid world premiere co-production; to Casey Childs, Andrew Leynse, Elliot Fox, Michelle Bossy, Tessa LaNeve, and Primary Stages for the smashing New York premiere; and especially to Terry Nolen, whose keen eye, clear head, and firm hand made the play shine in all three cities.

Finally, I would like to acknowledge the extraordinary efforts, enthusiasm, and generosity of Lee van de Velde, who has given so much of herself to the Arden for so long.

AUTHOR'S NOTES

Although the instruments referred to in the script must be real, the actors should not attempt to move their left hands along with the recorded passages indicated. This invariably looks fake, and will distract from the play. Bowing precisely with the right arm will convey sufficient verisimilitude while allowing the body to move naturally with the music; keeping the left hand relaxed and open renders the theatrical convention unambiguous: "We know we're not really playing."

Nevertheless, attention to correct posture and bowing form is essential in order to render the illusion that these musicians are masters in their field. Several intensive sessions with a string player/coach early on in rehearsals, followed by periodic check-ups, will insure that the actors are comfortable, confident, and convincing in their new professions.

Monologues in the play are sometimes underscored, but the four-part monologues should not be, as the alternating voices should create a music of their own.

Beats (short pauses) and pauses in the dialogue are as important as the rests in music. Please attend to them. When one character begins speaking before another has finished, the beginning of the overlap is marked with a slash (/). Thus, an actor with a slash in his or her line should ignore it and continue speaking without interruption, as it is merely a cue for the next speaker. A dash (—) indicates where one speaker is cut off by the next; an ellipsis (…) indicates where a speaker trails off, or searches for a word, and not an interruption.

NOTES ON PRODUCTION CD

Music selections provided on the production CD are indicated within stage directions in the script, e.g., "[CD track #19]." Occasionally, multiple options are included, e.g., "[CD track #10, 11, 12 or 13]."

Music required by the play but not included on the CD is indicated within the stage directions by "[Not included on CD]," and listed at the end of the script on the "Sound Effects" page.

Track #28 must immediately precede the dialogue at the top of Scene 13, as Dorian's opening lines refer explicitly to Grace's flat final note on this track. It is possible, however, to begin the scene with music excerpted from track #27 — i.e., a solo viola (Grace) practicing difficult passages before undertaking the final run [CD track #28], or overlapping violas at various volumes, suggesting a hallway full of musicians all practicing the same passage. In the latter example, overlapping violas would need to fade out as Grace's solo line [CD track #28, or the final moments of this track] take prominence.

OPUS was originally produced by Arden Theatre Company (Terrence J. Nolen, Producing Artistic Director; Amy Murphy, Managing Director) in Philadelphia, Pennsylvania, and City Theatre Company (Tracy Brigden, Artistic Director; Greg Quinlan, Managing Director) in Pittsburgh, Pennsylvania. The co-production opened in Philadelphia on January 12, 2006 and in Pittsburgh on March 17, 2006. It was directed by Terrence J. Nolen; the scenic design was by James Kronzer; the costume design was by Michael McAleer; the lighting design was by Andrew David Ostrowski; the sound design was by Jorge Cousineau; the dramaturg was Carlyn Aquiline; the assistant director was Georgia Schlessman; the production stage managers were Patricia G. Sabato (Arden) and Patti Kelly (City Theatre). The cast was as follows:

ELLIOT .... Patrick McNulty
ALAN .... Greg Wood
DORIAN .... David Whalen
CARL .... Douglas Rees
GRACE .... Erika Cuenca

OPUS received its New York premiere at Primary Stages (Casey Childs, Executive Producer; Andrew Leynse, Artistic Director; Elliot Fox, Managing Director) on July 24, 2007. It was directed by Terrence J. Nolen; the scenic design was by James Kronzer; the costume design was by Anne Kennedy; the lighting design was by Justin Townsend; the sound design was by Jorge Cousineau; the assistant director was Tessa LaNeve; the production stage manager was Fred Hemminger. The cast was as follows:

ELLIOT .... David Beach
ALAN .... Richard Topol
DORIAN .... Michael Laurence
GRACE .... Mahira Kakkar
CARL .... Douglas Rees

CHARACTERS

ELLIOT, forties. First violin.

ALAN, forties. Second violin.

DORIAN, forties. Viola.

CARL, forties. Cello.

GRACE, twenty-five. Viola.

SETTING

Various interiors in New York City, London, Pittsburgh, and Washington, D.C., most representable by four chairs and music stands. These elements could remain the same throughout, to emphasize the string quartet as a constant; or they could change, in order to make distinctions between different locations. (If the latter course is chosen, attention should be paid to making sure transitions are swift and unobtrusive, so as not to obstruct or slow the progression of scenes.)

TIME

Recently, and before that.

Opus runs ninety minutes and is performed without intermission.

OPUS

Prelude

As house lights fade, the sounds of a string quartet tuning. [CD track #1, 2 or 3.] Then, in darkness, the beginning of the "Alla danza tedesca" movement from Beethoven's Opus 130. [CD track #4.] Lights fade up on the Lazara String Quartet — Elliot, Alan, Carl and Dorian — each frozen in playing position.

As the musical phrase repeats, the four men begin "playing" along. The melody then breaks down, each man playing a piece and passing it along. All players join back in, though the music ends unresolved. Lights fade.

Scene 1

A pin spot illuminates each member of the Lazara Quartet as he begins speaking. All four face front, addressing an unseen interlocutor; each has a microphone clipped to his shirt. They are being interviewed individually by a documentary film-maker, and are therefore unaware of each other's comments.

CARL. "What is it?"
ALAN. *(Attaching his microphone.)* Why do I have to go first?
CARL. You mean, like a definition?
ALAN. You should start with Elliot.
ELLIOT. Let me see …

ALAN. He'll probably quote some French philosopher.
ELLIOT. I think Goethe said it best:
CARL. What is it …
ALAN. In the original language.
ELLIOT. "A discourse among four reasonable people."
ALAN. Carl will tell the joke …
CARL. Here's one:
ALAN. Though I've asked him to stop.
ELLIOT. Wonderful, isn't it?
CARL. "What's the definition of a string quartet?"
ELLIOT. Of course, it sounds better in German. *(Spot out on Elliot.)*
CARL. "One good violinist, one bad violinist, one former violinist, and someone who doesn't even like the violin."
ALAN. And Dorian …
DORIAN. What was the question again?
CARL. No — it's just a joke.
DORIAN. Right.
ALAN. God only knows.
CARL. Some of my best friends are violinists. *(Spot out on Carl.)*
ALAN. Dorian's … unpredictable. *(Spot out on Alan.)*
DORIAN. At its best … when everything's working right, when everyone's open to it, it's … *(As he searches for the word, music enters — the second theme from the "Cavatina" movement of Opus 130. [CD track #5 or 6.]Hearing it, he shuts his eyes with pleasure.)* lovemaking. *(He reexperiences the passage as it plays in his head:)* Elliot starts a phrase, maybe just a bit softer than usual, so we come in under, Alan and I, like we're … coddling it, like more than a breath would kill it. Then Carl lands on the bottom, terra firma, and the whole thing rises, floats, together, falls back, arches upward, no one leading, no one following, it's just … pulsating. Like it's alive, like some living, pulsing organism … *(Music disappears.)* Copulating with itself. *(Beat. Spot up on Alan.)*
ALAN. Me?
DORIAN. *(Opening his eyes.)* That sounds buggy, doesn't it?
ALAN. I was kind of hoping you'd forget about me …
DORIAN. You can edit that out.
ALAN. Okay, how about this: A string quartet is like a marriage, only with more fidelity.
DORIAN. Hmm?

ALAN. Actually, don't tell my wife I said that.
DORIAN. Oh. Right.
ALAN. She wouldn't understand. *(Spot out on Alan.)*
DORIAN. At its *worst* … it's like … *(He thinks. Long pause. Finding his answer, he looks out again.)* Swallowing Drano. *(Spot out on Dorian.)*

Scene 2

In darkness, a fragment from the discordant middle movement of Bartók's Second String Quartet. [CD track #7 or 8.] Lights rise on the quartet, minus Dorian, as they play the last four bars. In his place sits Grace, roughly twenty years their junior. After the final chord, they remain still for a moment, bows poised above the strings. Then they relax into the afterglow.

ELLIOT. Well. That was …
ALAN. Well done.
ELLIOT. Bracing.
GRACE. Thanks.
CARL. Bravo.
GRACE. I missed a few notes.
ELLIOT. No, you didn't.
GRACE. Well, almost.
ALAN. Almost doesn't count.
ELLIOT. Did you study it with Krenski?
GRACE. "It?"
CARL. The Bartok.
GRACE. Oh; no.
ELLIOT. But you've played it before.
GRACE. No, never. *(Pause.)*
ALAN. This was your first time?
GRACE. I'm sorry.
ELLIOT. No apologies necessary.
GRACE. I did listen to the recording.
CARL. Whose?

GRACE. Well, yours.
ELLIOT. Oh, God …
GRACE. Should I not have?
ALAN. No, that's fine. We just don't take it that slow anymore.
GRACE. So I noticed … *(They all share a chuckle. Pause. Elliot pulls out a sheet of paper from behind his music.)*
ELLIOT. You play better than you should. *(Beat.)*
GRACE. I don't know what that means.
ELLIOT. Your resume's not particularly impressive.
GRACE. Oh.
ELLIOT. In fact, it looks like a hundred others we got from starry-eyed grad students: padded with *music camps,* awards from *high school* …
ALAN. Church gigs …
ELLIOT. *(Reading from the resume.)* "Concerto soloist with the *Weehawken Youth Symphony* … "
GRACE. I didn't see it as "padding" …
CARL. Of course not.
GRACE. It's just what I've done.
ELLIOT. *All I'm saying is,* if Krenski hadn't called you the best student he's had in twenty-five years, you wouldn't be sitting here. *(Beat.)*
GRACE. He said that?
ALAN. Not in so many words.
CARL. *Forty*-five years.
ALAN. Good God, how old is he?
CARL. Ancient. He was ancient when we were there.
ELLIOT. And if you hadn't also exceeded our expectations today, we wouldn't be having this conversation. We'd be saying nice things and asking about your pets as we push you out the door. Am I right, gentlemen?
CARL. Yes.
ELLIOT. Alan?
ALAN. Yep.
ELLIOT. Good. *(Beat. Back to Grace:)* So. Congratulations.
GRACE. *(Uncertain.)* Oh. Thanks.
ELLIOT. Can you start tomorrow? *(Beat.)*
GRACE. What?
ELLIOT. We like to rehearse first thing in the morning.
CARL. First thing being ten-thirty.
ALAN. After the coffee kicks in.

GRACE. Um …
CARL. Usually we take turns hosting,
ELLIOT. One day, Carl's spacious brownstone,
ALAN. The next, my squalid, miserable hovel.
CARL. The host is responsible for snacks.
ELLIOT. Do you have four chairs?
GRACE. Um … yes, but —
ELLIOT. Good.
GRACE. One's actually more of a bean bag …
CARL. I'll bring my own.
GRACE. Did … something just happen that I wasn't aware of? *(Beat.)*
ELLIOT. We just hired you.
GRACE. That's what I thought.
ALAN. Did it seem abrupt?
GRACE. Well, yeah.
CARL. We work fast.
GRACE. I mean, don't you want to talk it over?
ELLIOT. We did.
ALAN. You just didn't notice.
CARL. That's how we talk:
ALAN. In shorthand. *(Long pause.)*
ELLIOT. At this point, one would expect you to say, "I'm thrilled," or words to that effect.
GRACE. I'm thrilled, I am, really, this is …
ALAN. "A dream come true," "the opportunity of a lifetime"…?
GRACE. Can I think it over? *(Pause. They weren't expecting this.)*
CARL. Sure.
ALAN. Of course.
ELLIOT. I'll be home all night, call as late as you want.
GRACE. I meant, for a few days. *(Beat.)*
CARL. Days?
GRACE. I have an audition on Thursday.
ELLIOT. For what?
GRACE. The Pittsburgh Symphony.
ALAN. *Pittsburgh?*
GRACE. It's a principal position.
ALAN. You don't want to play for Pittsburgh.
GRACE. They have an excellent orchestra …
ALAN. Maybe for Pittsburgh.

ELLIOT. Pittsburgh's not the point. Do you really want to spend your professional life in thrall to a baton?
GRACE. "In thrall"?
ELLIOT. The Midwest tours, the obligatory Fourth of July concerts …
ALAN. Playing Beethoven's Fifth for the hundred and nineteenth time …
GRACE. Okay, but —
ELLIOT. We're giving you the opportunity to be one of four equal voices. Playing the greatest chamber —
CARL. Elliot …
ELLIOT. The job satisfaction rates for orchestra players are actually lower than *dentists.*
CARL. Elliot.
ELLIOT. The suicide rates are *higher.*
CARL. *Stop. (Pause.)*
GRACE. I'm sorry, I — This is all very flattering, I'm very flattered. I never expected you would just … *(Pause.)* I need to take this audition. If you can wait till next week —
ELLIOT. We can't.
ALAN. What if she —
ELLIOT. I said we can't. *(Pause.)*
GRACE. Then I'm afraid I'll have to say no. *(Pause. Elliot nods slightly.)* I'm sorry. *(Grace quickly packs her instrument in its case. Alan breaks the silence:)*
ALAN. Thanks for coming in.
GRACE. Oh, thanks for seeing me — hearing me, whatever. I've wanted to be in a professional quartet since, well, since I heard you all play. But …
ELLIOT. *(Completing her thought.)* Pittsburgh beckons.
GRACE. Right. Well. *(She stands.)* Thanks again.
ALAN. Goodbye. *(Elliot shows her out. Alan and Carl just sit there until he returns. Then:)* Why did you do that?
ELLIOT. What?
ALAN. You always do that.
ELLIOT. What are / you —
ALAN. Turn everything into a fucking ultimatum.
ELLIOT. *She wanted us to wait till next week, can we wait till next week? (Pause. They all know they cannot.)*
ALAN. Shit. *(Pause.)* What do we do now?

CARL. Go to our B list.
ELLIOT. We don't have a B list.
ALAN. What about Kirchner?
ELLIOT. C-minus.
CARL. Deak?
ELLIOT. With *that* vibrato? *(He flops his left wrist flaccidly back and forth. Pause.)*
ALAN. Richard wasn't awful.
ELLIOT. Richard's an automaton.
CARL. He can play the notes.
ELLIOT. That's precisely the problem. He doesn't make music, he *extrudes* notes. It's like trying to make love with a kitchen appliance.
ALAN. Then I don't know who to go to.
CARL. Manzer, Tomasetti …
ELLIOT. No.
CARL. The guy with the hair …
ALAN. They're none of them as good as her.
CARL. Not even as good as Richard.
ELLIOT. Who's not good enough. Besides, he's got a cat.
ALAN. So?
ELLIOT. *So?* You know how I get.
CARL. So we don't have to rehearse there. *(Beat.)*
ALAN. We don't have a choice, El. I think it's Richard or nobody. *(Pause. Elliot sighs.)*
ELLIOT. What's his number? *(Alan goes to retrieve it from his violin case. Elliot gets a portable phone.)*
CARL. Have you ever actually tried making love with a kitchen appliance?
ELLIOT. Who I sleep with and whether it plugs in is none of your business.
ALAN. I once had a fling with my toaster, but I had to end it. *(He hands a folded piece of paper to Elliot.)*
CARL. Molly catch you in the act?
ALAN. No, I just kept popping out before I was done. *(Carl is amused. Elliot gives them a look of reproach, then locates the number on the sheet and presses the appropriate buttons. They wait in silence for someone to answer. Finally:)*
ELLIOT. *(To phone.)* Gloria, hi, it's Elliot Barr, is Richard about? *(Pause.)* Really? "Waiting for our call," that's great. *(He looks at the others. The doorbell buzzes.)* Thanks, dear. *(To Alan.)* Can you get

that? *(Alan exits; Elliot calls after him:)* And if it's a fat kid raising money for cripples, tell him I changed my mind. *(To Carl.)* This kid won't take no for an answer, he comes back day after day till you'll promise him anything just to get *(To phone.)* Richard, hi, glad I caught you. *(Pause.)* So Gloria said. Listen, I've got some excellent news. *(Alan reenters.)*

ALAN. Don't. *(Elliot turns to look at him. Grace comes in behind Alan, looking a little sheepish. Beat.)*

ELLIOT. Uh … yeah, listen, Richard, could you … hold on a minute? Thanks. *(He covers the mouthpiece with his hand. Everyone looks at Grace. Pause.)* Yes?

GRACE. I changed my mind. *(Beat.)*

ELLIOT. Changed your mind.

GRACE. If you still want me. *(Beat.)* On the way down I realized you're right, I don't want to play in an orchestra, I never really enjoyed it. Pittsburgh just sounded like a real job, well, the prospect of a real job, playing with one of the biggies, you know, with a pension and sick days, dental insurance. *(Beat.)* Of course, even as I say this, I realize I never actually asked you if you had dental insurance …

CARL. We do.

GRACE. Oh. Okay. Then I was just being stupid. See, the thing is, I need to make a living at this. I can't go crawling home and say, "You were right all along, it was unrealistic, I should have gone to law school like you said." I know that's more than you need to know, but — Well, anyway, if there's still time to accept, I'd like to. Very much. *(Pause. Elliot looks to Carl, who nods, then to Alan, who nods. He looks at the phone in his hand, then reluctantly holds it to his mouth again.)*

ELLIOT. Richard, still there? *(Beat.)* Listen, sorry about that. My … upstairs neighbor had a … pet emergency. *(Beat.)* Yeah, Schnauzer, irritable bowels, big mess, anyway, where was I? *(Pause.)* Right, "excellent news" … *(He rolls his eyes at the others.) Listen,* Richard, the boys and I have come to a decision about Dorian's replacement. *(Beat.)* And it's somebody else. *(Pause.)* Somebody other than you. *(Pause.)* Right. I can see how prefacing that with "excellent news" might have been misleading. *(Pause.)* I know, I'm sorry. *(Pause.)* Of course. *(Pause.)* Right. *(Pause.)* Of course. *(To Alan, hand over mouthpiece:)* Ring the doorbell. *(Alan exits. To phone.)* Right. *(Beat.)* Understandably. *(The doorbell buzzes.)* Oh my god, she's back with the Schnauzer. Listen, Richard, gotta go, thanks for coming in, I'm sorry it didn't work out, but maybe this new violist will crack up, too,

and if so, you'll be the first one we call, okay? Right, bye. *(He hangs up, looks at the phone. Beat.)* That could have gone better.
GRACE. I'm sorry.
ELLIOT. And you can stop apologizing. It's an annoying habit and only slows down our work.
GRACE. I'm — Okay.
ELLIOT. Here's what you need to know: *(He sets the phone aside.)* The Lazara Quartet is built on consensus. Everyone gets a vote; we all have veto power. If three of us want to play the Kreisler and you think the Kreisler's "a rancid piece of sentimental schlock,"
ALAN. To quote your predecessor …
ELLIOT. Then we don't play the Kreisler, it's that simple. The only time your opinion's moot is when we decide to fire you.
CARL. If.
ALAN. *If* we decide to fire you.
CARL. And that's not going to happen.
ELLIOT. Of course not. Because you're smart, and charming, and *sane,* and exceptionally gifted.
GRACE. Thank you.
ELLIOT. And those are the last complimentary words you're going to hear. Because if we wasted our rehearsals patting each other on the fanny, we'd never get any work done. *(Alan removes a small white envelope from his music stand.)*
ALAN. Have you ever been to the White House?
GRACE. The White House?
ELLIOT. It's where the president lives.
GRACE. We went on a field trip in fourth grade, but I threw up in the China Room and missed the tour.
CARL. Well, you're going back. *(Alan hands the envelope to Grace. She looks at the others, then pulls out an engraved invitation.)*
GRACE. *(Reading it.)* Oh my god …
ALAN. The ceremony's going to be televised.
GRACE. *(Still reading.)* Wow.
ALAN. All of it, even us.
CARL. Fifteen million viewers.
ELLIOT. If we play splendidly, it will prove to the world — our critics, our … detractors, those who would love to see us fail — that the Lazara Quartet is alive and well.
GRACE. I didn't vote for him. Either term. Is that all right?
ELLIOT. None of us voted for him, dear, he's a pig.

ALAN. Dorian's mother.
ELLIOT. Mothers of former members don't count.
CARL. Still, fifteen million viewers …
ALAN. *(Taking the invitation.)* It's an opportunity.
ELLIOT. A *rare* opportunity …
GRACE. *(To Alan.)* The "opportunity of a lifetime"? *(He smiles at the reference.)*
ELLIOT. Precisely. *(He stands. To all:)* Gentlemen, get a good night's sleep. In six days, Lazara rises from the dead! *(Alan and Carl move to pack up their instruments. Aside, to Grace:)* And this time …
GRACE. Yes?
ELLIOT. Don't throw up in the China Room. *(He turns to pack up his violin. Lights fade.)*

Scene 3

Music: the "Largo" from Bach's Concerto in D Minor for Two Violins. [CD track #9.] Lights rise on Elliot and Dorian, in pin spots. They are being interviewed separately, though they have been asked the same question.

ELLIOT. Chemistry.
DORIAN. Oh, I don't know …
ELLIOT. It's chemistry.
DORIAN. I'm tempted to say it's chemistry.
ELLIOT. And hard work.
DORIAN. But I have a complex history with chemicals.
ELLIOT. Luck, too, I suppose. Though I don't believe in luck.
DORIAN. We met at Curtis.
ELLIOT. Dorian, Alan and I all studied with Reinhold Schnell.
DORIAN. Our teacher was a Nazi.
ELLIOT. A real taskmaster.
DORIAN. Literally — straight from the Third Reich.
ELLIOT. But he had an ear for talent.
DORIAN. We were only allowed to study works by Aryan composers.

ELLIOT. In our last year, he asked Dorian and me to play the Bach Concerto for Two Violins.
DORIAN. Which is how we came together. *(The music rises in volume, both men "listening" to it in their memories. The orchestra fades away, leaving only the solo violin parts.)*
ELLIOT. I'll never forget the Largo.
DORIAN. In the slow movement,
ELLIOT. One of us,
DORIAN. I don't remember who played first,
ELLIOT. Would enter with that simple,
DORIAN. Tender,
ELLIOT. Lyrical theme,
DORIAN. And when the other came in,
ELLIOT. The tones matched so well,
ELLIOT and DORIAN. You couldn't tell who was who anymore.
ELLIOT. First one on top,
DORIAN. Like lovers rolling,
ELLIOT. Then the other,
DORIAN. Rolling …
ELLIOT. Until you lose all awareness of who's who,
ELLIOT and DORIAN. And there's just … *(Music out.)*
ELLIOT. Music. *(Beat. Elliot opens his eyes.)* That was it. *(Dorian opens his eyes, still pained by the memory.)*
DORIAN. That was the start of everything. *(Lights fade.)*

Scene 4

Music: the final seconds of the third ("Allegro") movement of Bach's Concerto for Two Violins. [Not included on CD.] Lights rise on Alan's apartment, where Alan stands, rumpled, hair a mess, wearing a bathrobe. Grace stands before him, freshly scrubbed, viola case in hand.

GRACE. I'm early.
ALAN. Yeah.
GRACE. I'm sorry.

ALAN. That's okay.
GRACE. You can blame it on my dad: "Early is on time, on time is late."
ALAN. Your dad would be proud. *(Grace sets down her case.)*
GRACE. This isn't so bad.
ALAN. Huh?
GRACE. You called your place squalid and miserable.
ALAN. Ah. Well. *(Looking around:)* I guess miserable's in the eye of the beholder.
GRACE. Do you want me to go away and come back?
ALAN. No, that's okay.
GRACE. So you can get dressed?
ALAN. I just need to pour a cup of coffee. Over my head. *(He starts out.)* You want some?
GRACE. Do you have tea?
ALAN. *(Uncertainly.)* Yeah …
GRACE. I'll have Red Zinger.
ALAN. Uh …
GRACE. Or Wild Berry.
ALAN. I don't have those.
GRACE. Any kind of Zinger, then: Lemon …
ALAN. No Zingers.
GRACE. Oh. Mandarin Orange?
ALAN. Sorry.
GRACE. Peppermint, Spearmint…? *(He shakes his head.)* Okay. What do you have?
ALAN. I've got a little bag with the word "Tea" written on it in Dutch.
GRACE. Oh.
ALAN. At least, I think it's Dutch. I swiped a bunch from our hotel in Amsterdam, just in case somebody someday asked me for tea.
GRACE. That'll be fine. *(He exits. Grace begins looking around the apartment.)* When did you play in Amsterdam?
ALAN. *(Offstage.)* I don't know — six months ago? Six years ago? It all starts to run together.
GRACE. I've heard it's beautiful.
ALAN. *(Offstage.)* It probably was. *(Grace looks at a photograph on the "fourth wall." Alan reenters with a mug of coffee.)* I'll never forget the Concertgebouw, though — best acoustics in the world. You play a chord there, it goes on forever.

GRACE. She's pretty. *(Beat.)*
ALAN. It's an old picture. *(Beat.)*
GRACE. She's not pretty anymore?
ALAN. No, Molly's always pretty. She just doesn't look at me like that anymore.
GRACE. You were married?
ALAN. Seven years. Like the itch.
GRACE. The itch? *(He shrugs, pleading guilty.)* Oh.
ALAN. Life on the road, it's … lonely. You'll see. It's all very exciting at first — jetting to far-off places, soaking up adulation from strangers in languages you don't understand, but … After a while, it feels like all you ever do is go from a plane to a car to a hall to a hotel to a car to a plane and start all over again. So, if you're lucky enough to find another human being along the way — on the plane, at the hall, or, please God, in the hotel — well … it helps you remember you're not a piece of luggage. *(He looks at her. An awkward pause.)*
GRACE. Um, it's hot. *(Beat.)*
ALAN. Hmm?
GRACE. Your tea kettle? *(Sure enough, a now barely audible whistle can be heard offstage.)*
ALAN. Oh. Right. *(He exits.)*
GRACE. It actually whistles. That's quaint.
ALAN. *(Offstage.)* Is it?
GRACE. I've always wanted a kettle that whistles.
ALAN. *(Offstage.)* Well, it's got a pretty limited repertoire. *(He reenters with a second mug.)* I've tried to teach it the "Colonel Bogey March," but it's got no ear. Milk or sugar?
GRACE. No, thanks.
ALAN. Good, 'cause I don't have either. Mud in your eye. *(They clink mugs, he drinks. She checks her watch, letting the tea bag steep.)*
GRACE. Are the others usually late?
ALAN. No. Carl's up at dawn with his kids and Elliot's pathologically punctual, like you.
GRACE. "Pathologically punctual"?
ALAN. Did I say that?
GRACE. You did.
ALAN. Forgive me. I'm pathologically late. *(He drinks. She looks around again, more agitated this time. He observes her closely.)* You don't have to be scared, you know.

GRACE. Easy for you to say.
ALAN. You already got the job.
GRACE. Yeah, but — I don't know — lashing myself to three perfect strangers …
ALAN. Oh, we're far from perfect.
GRACE. Well, that's just it! I mean, I've heard there are quarrels, that things get personal sometimes —
ALAN. Ah.
GRACE. Even violent.
ALAN. You've been watching the documentary. *(Beat.)*
GRACE. I rented it last night.
ALAN. Carl's famous quote about "the threat of physical injury"?
GRACE. He was exaggerating, right? *(He does not respond.)* Oh God …
ALAN. But there's a huge difference between *saying* you're going to rip someone's head off and —
GRACE. Somebody said that?
ALAN. Probably all of us. *(She takes this in.)* But nobody's done it. *(Beat.)* Yet. *(He drinks.)*
GRACE. Now you're *trying* to make me nervous.
ALAN. Dorian once broke my bow in half.
GRACE. That's awful!
ALAN. Not my good bow.
GRACE. Still.
ALAN. My good bow was being rehaired.
GRACE. What possessed him to do that?
ALAN. We were performing K. 590 in Brussels and I played a passage off the string instead of on.
GRACE. So he *broke* your bow?
ALAN. He waited till we were backstage …
GRACE. I don't understand. *(Pause.)*
ALAN. Dorian felt things more deeply than most people. That's what made him brilliant — visionary, really. Sometimes you got the sense he was getting it piped in from — No, that sounds like it was canned, it wasn't, just the opposite. It was like he was … conversing with Mozart, like the composer was making it up on the spot and it was just coming out, no intermediary, direct from the source, it was … *(He pauses, searching for the word.)*
GRACE. Wonderful. *(Beat.)*
ALAN. Terrifying. *(Beat.)* And extraordinary.

GRACE. Then why did you make him play viola? *(He just looks at her.)* Either you or Elliot could have.
ALAN. Well, you saw the documentary: "He / lost the — "
GRACE. *(Overlapping after /.)* " … lost the coin toss," right, but that doesn't make sense, not if he was visionary. Shouldn't he have been first violin? *(Beat.)*
ALAN. Do you really want Joan of Arc as your leader? Giving cues, setting tempos? I mean, she's inspirational, sure, sometimes she takes you to a whole new place. But when you're sitting down to play a sold-out concert in Carnegie Hall … do you really want to wonder if tonight that person's talking to dead people? *(Grace sips her tea.)* So, we settled. For a little less brilliance, less spontaneity, maybe. But a lot more reliability.
GRACE. Do you think he's killed himself? *(Alan reacts.)* I'm sorry, I just — I've heard rumors. Stuff online? People say he had a history of —
ALAN. I'm aware of the history.
GRACE. So … do you think they're true?
ALAN. I'm hoping not.
GRACE. But you don't know. *(Beat.)*
ALAN. I've called, emailed, stopped by … It's like he's dropped off the face of the earth.
GRACE. Then … he really might / have —
ALAN. I'd rather not go there. *(She nods. Pause.)* How's your tea?
GRACE. What? *(He points to her mug.)* Oh — um, it's not. *(Beat.)*
ALAN. Not what?
GRACE. Tea. *(Pause.)*
ALAN. What is it?
GRACE. I don't know, but it's definitely not tea. *(Beat. He holds out his hand; she hands him the mug. He sips, considers.)* See?
ALAN. God, I hope it wasn't pot.
GRACE. Pot?
ALAN. That would be such a waste …
GRACE. How could it be pot?
ALAN. You never know in Amsterdam. *(He hands back the mug; she looks at it with suspicion. Alan takes a drink of coffee. Grace sets her mug down.)*
GRACE. Maybe they forgot to change their clocks …
ALAN. I doubt it. *(Beat.)*
GRACE. I set mine ahead before I go to sleep, just to be on the

safe side.
ALAN. Back.
GRACE. Hmm?
ALAN. "Spring forward, Fall back." *(Long pause. Grace stares at Alan, then at her watch, then back at him.)*
GRACE. Oh my God.
ALAN. Don't worry about it.
GRACE. I'm two hours early.
ALAN. Like I said, your dad would be proud.
GRACE. I am *so* sorry …
ALAN. Forget it.
GRACE. Why didn't you tell me? *(Beat.)*
ALAN. Change of pace. I usually have to wake up alone. *(She smiles, embarrassed.)*
GRACE. Well — I should go.
ALAN. No.
GRACE. Give you a chance to shower, get dressed.
ALAN. Stick around, have another cup of ganja.
GRACE. I won't get in the way?
ALAN. Not unless you're standing on the bath mat. *(She smiles, sits, and starts to unpack her viola. He drains his mug and starts off. As he disappears:)*
GRACE. Alan? *(He returns. Pause.)* Why did you fire him? *(Pause.)*
ALAN. Elliot felt he'd crossed a line.
GRACE. Crossed a line how?
ALAN. Grace.
GRACE. What?
ALAN. You're going to be fine.
GRACE. I know.
ALAN. No, really. Forget about Pittsburgh and law school. Trust me, it's going to be fine. *(Beat.)*
GRACE. *(Unconvinced.)* Yeah. *(Alan exits. Lights fade.)*

Scene 5

Music: the two solo lines from the opening movement of Bach's Concerto in D minor for Two Violins, now played by violin and viola. [CD track #10 ,11 ,12 or 13.] Lights rise to reveal Elliot and Dorian, who has just entered.

ELLIOT. Where have you been?
DORIAN. I told you, having lunch with a friend of Mother's.
ELLIOT. For twelve hours?
DORIAN. Cocktails, followed by a goat cheese tartlet, Japanese miso with soba noodles —
ELLIOT. I don't need to know the menu.
DORIAN. There was even a cheese platter.
ELLIOT. We've talked about this. It doesn't work.
DORIAN. What?
ELLIOT. When I don't know where you are, whom you're with …
DORIAN. You didn't think I was playing duets with somebody else…?
ELLIOT. Well, you leave at nine, come back at eight-thirty —
DORIAN. Sorry. I'd've come home sooner, but the train was late.
ELLIOT. What train?
DORIAN. From Boston. God, now I'm starving — can you believe it? *(He exits through an interior door.)*
ELLIOT. Boston?
DORIAN. *(Offstage.)* Well, that's where she lives.
ELLIOT. Who?
DORIAN. *(Offstage.)* Mrs. Van Nuys — well, "Lydia" now.
ELLIOT. You went to Boston for *lunch?*
DORIAN. *(Offstage.)* I know, but she wanted to give them to me in person.
ELLIOT. Give you what?
DORIAN. *(Reappearing.)* I thought you'd never ask. *(He exits where he first entered, returning immediately holding an instrument case in each hand. Elliot looks at them in bewilderment.)*
ELLIOT. What are these?

DORIAN. Matching bowling balls. I thought we needed a hobby.
ELLIOT. *Will you be serious?*
DORIAN. See for yourself. *(He sets the cases down. Elliot looks at him, then opens the smaller first, revealing a violin. He is speechless.)* She said, "Any quartet calling itself Lazara should be playing Lazaras." And I had to agree. *(Elliot quickly opens the other case.)* They're a matched set — violin/viola. Unbelievable sound. I tried them both, right there in the restaurant. Somebody gave me a tip. *(He produces a bill from his shirt pocket, then replaces it. Beat. Elliot looks up at him.)* They're ours.
ELLIOT. She's lending them to us?
DORIAN. She gave them to us. *(Beat.)*
ELLIOT. I don't understand.
DORIAN. She heard us at Jordan Hall last month. Apparently the Opus Ninety-five did her in.
ELLIOT. She's *giving* them to us?
DORIAN. Well, that and my boyish charm, of course.
ELLIOT. *(Overwhelmed.)* Oh my god …
DORIAN. You may be familiar with the boyish charm …
ELLIOT. You — are *incorrigible! (He kisses him impulsively.)*
DORIAN. *(Half to himself.)* I get the job done, though, don't I?
ELLIOT. *(Removing the violin from its case.)* They're … exquisite. Gorgeous! I don't even — *(Beat.)* We should call the boys. *(He stands.)*
DORIAN. Before we do —
ELLIOT. No, you're right — let's play something first.
DORIAN. Nelly …
ELLIOT. Mozart duets?
DORIAN. Nell.
ELLIOT. What. *(Beat.)*
DORIAN. I was wondering. *(Beat.)*
ELLIOT. Yes? *(Beat.)*
DORIAN. Maybe we could switch off now and then. *(Beat.)*
ELLIOT. Switch off?
DORIAN. In the quartet. I play violin, you play viola. *(Beat.)* Once in a while.
ELLIOT. I don't think that's a good idea.
DORIAN. Other quartets switch off.
ELLIOT. I know, / but —
DORIAN. For equality's sake.

ELLIOT. We agreed.
DORIAN. *You* agreed. Ten years ago. Don't you think —
ELLIOT. It's better this way. *(Beat.)* Really.
DORIAN. Better for whom?
ELLIOT. All four of us. *(Beat.)*
DORIAN. I just think —
ELLIOT. Look, let's not rock the boat. *(He takes Dorian's head in his hand.)* All right? Things are fine the way they are. Better than fine. And now — my god! With these? *(He lifts the viola out of its case to hold up both instruments.)* Wait till we tell the boys, they'll — Well, not Carl, he couldn't care less, but Alan … *(He hands Dorian the viola.)* Come on, let's call them together.
DORIAN. You call them. *(Beat.)*
ELLIOT. You don't want to call them? *(Beat. Dorian looks up.)*
DORIAN. You call. *(Pause. Elliot puts his hand on Dorian's shoulder.)*
ELLIOT. Trust me. It's better this way. *(He exits with the violin. Dorian looks down at the viola in his hands. Lights fade.)*

Scene 6

Music: Pachelbel's Canon in D Major. [CD track #14 or 15.] It's simple and tuneful, if a little boring. Lights rise on Elliot, Alan, Grace and Carl rehearsing. After a moment, Elliot stops, unable to continue.

ELLIOT. Ugh! This is too much … *(The others stop.)*
CARL. What?
ELLIOT. Too little, really.
ALAN. Let's just —
ELLIOT. It's dinner music. Bland, innocuous. Designed not to draw attention away from the beef bourguignon.
ALAN. It's what they asked for.
CARL. Who?
ALAN. I don't know, the president, first lady …
ELLIOT. Only because they're Philistines.
CARL. Who told you this is what they wanted?

ALAN. The girl.
ELLIOT. What girl?
ALAN. The *girl,* from the White House.
ELLIOT. Well, it sounds like a tampon commercial.
CARL. *(Aware of Grace's presence.)* Elliot.
GRACE. At least they didn't ask for "Hail to the Chief." *(Carl chuckles.)*
ELLIOT. Thank God for small favors. *(He lifts his instrument to play again.)*
ALAN. Actually, they did. *(The others look at him.)*
CARL. Get out.
ALAN. Just once, when the president enters.
ELLIOT. You're joking.
ALAN. They sent me the parts. *(He pulls some additional pages from behind his sheet music.)*
CARL. Oh, Christ.
ELLIOT. We're not playing it.
ALAN. We have to!
CARL. Why?
ALAN. Because they asked. And they're giving us fifteen million viewers. And none of you were willing to be the liaison, so I told them we would. *(Beat.)*
ELLIOT. Then I'm not playing the tampon ad. *(Elliot removes the music from his stand and drops it onto the floor.)*
ALAN. El …
ELLIOT. If they want Muzak, they can hire the Mantovani Strings. *(Beat. Alan looks to Carl for support, but he simply shrugs. Back to Elliot:)*
ALAN. And what am I supposed to tell them?
ELLIOT. Tell them this: "A minor work by a minor composer is only fitting for a minor president."
CARL. Ouch.
ELLIOT. "A major statesman — "
ALAN. Oh, please …
ELLIOT. "*A major statesman* requires a masterpiece. A work of *substance.*"
CARL. At which point we suggest…? *(Beat.)*
ELLIOT. Opus One-thirty-one. *(Beat.)*
ALAN. There's no way.
ELLIOT. Why not?

ALAN. It's too long for one thing.
GRACE. Opus One thirty-one?
CARL. Beethoven.
ELLIOT. You know it?
GRACE. I know of it, but I've never played it.
ELLIOT. How I envy you.
ALAN. We can't do it.
ELLIOT. Of course we can.
ALAN. It's too long.
CARL. Too long, too strange, too dark …
ALAN. Too soon.
CARL. Besides, for us, it's bad luck.
ELLIOT. It's the greatest quartet ever written. *(Pause. They know he's right.)* It's the best there is, and we can play the piss out of it.
CARL. We've only got five days.
ELLIOT. She can do it.
ALAN. They're giving us twenty-five minutes, tops.
ELLIOT. With or without "Hail to the Chief"?
ALAN. One thirty-one lasts forty.
ELLIOT. We'll play fast.
ALAN. El …
ELLIOT. We'll play fast and they'll let us, because it's a monumental work. *(Beat.)* Carl? *(Pause.)*
CARL. Yeah, okay.
ELLIOT. Grace?
GRACE. What.
CARL. We're voting.
GRACE. Oh. Sure.
ELLIOT. Alan? *(Pause.)*
ALAN. All right, I'll pitch it to them.
ELLIOT. Don't pitch it — sell it.
ALAN. But we're going to have to play "Hail to the Chief."
CARL. Oh, god …
ALAN. As a concession.
ELLIOT. Do I have to play it well?
ALAN. Like you voted for him.
CARL. One thirty-one it is.
ELLIOT. Where are the parts?
ALAN. Buried in a box. *(He gets up, places his violin back in its case.)*
CARL. I'm gonna need coffee … *(He sets his cello down and*

stands.)

ALAN. It's on. *(He starts out.)*

ELLIOT. Do you have tea?

ALAN. That depends on what you call tea. *(He shares a glance with Grace, who chuckles as he exits.)*

CARL. Christ, I'll bet it's that shit from the Netherlands …

ELLIOT. *(Calling off.)* I'll pass. *(Carl exits to the kitchen. Elliot and Grace remain seated with their instruments, Grace somewhat stiffly. After a long pause:)* So — having fun yet?

GRACE. Yes.

ELLIOT. Really?

GRACE. Yes!

ELLIOT. Well, this too shall pass. *(Pause.)* You'll like the Beethoven.

GRACE. I'm sure.

ELLIOT. It's a masterpiece.

GRACE. So you said.

ELLIOT. What I wouldn't give to play it for the first time. *(Pause. He considers her for a moment, then:)* I'd like you to try something. *(He gets up with his violin and squats by an instrument case on the floor.)*

GRACE. Okay …

ELLIOT. Only if you want to. The others said not now, not yet, but I say what's the harm?

GRACE. What is it? *(Elliot turns, holding a viola in his other hand.)*

ELLIOT. His viola. *(Grace does not respond.)* Well, not his. It belongs to the quartet. Like my violin. Lazara made them both in 1710 from the same wood — literally the same tree. You can trace the grain from one to the other. *(He holds them side by side for her to examine.)* The timbres match so well, it's obvious they were meant to be played together. *(She studies the viola; he studies her.)* Go on — try it. *(She puts her own viola into its case and accepts the Lazara, placing it under her chin.)* Too big?

GRACE. No. No, it's good. *(Grace begins playing the "Prelude" of Bach's G Major Suite for Unaccompanied Cello, transcribed for viola. [CD track #16 or 17.] After a few seconds, drawn by the instrument's familiar sound, Carl enters, unseen by Grace, holding a coffee mug.)*

CARL. I thought we agreed —

ELLIOT. She wanted to try it. *(Grace has stopped playing.)*

CARL. You mean *you* wanted —

ELLIOT. I said, "Wouldn't you like to try it?" She said yes. I didn't

hold a gun to her head. *(Grace holds the viola out to Elliot.)*
GRACE. It's beautiful.
ELLIOT. You can play it if you want.
GRACE. I did.
ELLIOT. With the quartet.
CARL. You don't have to.
ELLIOT. *(To Carl.)* I said "if you *want.*"
CARL. Who cares what name's on the label? She should play what she's comfortable playing.
ELLIOT. Then let her be the judge of that. *(Carl and Elliot stare at each other for a moment, then simultaneously look to Grace for her response. Beat.)*
GRACE. I'd like to try it. *(Elliot turns to Carl with a "There, you see?" look. Carl ignores this and returns to his chair. Alan enters, music in hand.)*
ALAN. Sorry it took me so long. Somebody mixed them in with the Opus Eighteens.
ELLIOT. "Somebody"?
ALAN. Well, I'm somebody, aren't I? *(He hands out parts. To Grace:)* You can ignore the fingerings. Dorian had a weird way of squirreling around the fingerboard that was uniquely his. *(He retrieves his violin.)*
ELLIOT. From the top?
CARL. Let's do it. *(All raise their instruments except Alan, who has finally noticed Dorian's viola.)*
ALAN. *(To Elliot.)* Why is she playing —
GRACE. It's okay.
ALAN. Carl, didn't we agree —
ELLIOT. She said she wanted to try it, so we're trying it. For the blend. *(He smiles at Grace. Alan looks to Carl, who shrugs.)* Best of all, since it's played Opus One-thirty-one before, it already knows the notes. So: *(He places his bow on the string.) Molto espressivo* — feel it in two ... *(He begins playing a mournful solo line, then is joined a few bars later by Alan. [CD track #18.] Lights fade.)*

Scene 7

The music continues in the darkness. A pin spot rises on Carl as the cello line enters the fugue. The music fades but continues at a low volume underneath his "interview."

CARL. Maybe, but I don't like to argue. Ask my kids. They know if I find them fighting over the remote, I'm liable to break the damn thing in half. Ask them — I've done it. Twice. See, I don't have time for petty squabbling. Once you have cancer, even if you kick it, knock wood, *(He knocks on his cello.)* your clock ticks a little bit louder. That's not a bad thing; that's a good thing. Keeps life in focus, priorities straight: tick-tick-tick-tick-tick-tick-tick … STILL, in any ensemble, there's naturally going to be disagreements. People think when you're a quartet it's got to be rosy-cozy all the time — no. With four opinions in the room, four passionate individuals, sometimes tempers flare.
DORIAN. *(In darkness.)* For Christ's sake, Nelly …
CARL. Now and then words may fly.
DORIAN. *(In darkness.)* You sound like shit there.
ELLIOT. *(In darkness.)* Will you shut up?
CARL. Occasionally, there might be a hint of violence.
DORIAN. *(In darkness.)* Jesus, listen to you …
ALAN. *(In darkness.)* Dorian …
CARL. Even the threat of physical injury.
DORIAN. *(In darkness.)* You're playing like a retarded fourth-grader …
ELLIOT. *(In darkness.)* I swear, if he says another / word, I'm going to —
ALAN. *(In darkness. Overlapping after / .)* Ignore him.
DORIAN. *(In darkness.)* What'll you do?
ALAN. *(In darkness.)* Stop it, / both of you!
ELLIOT. *(In darkness. Overlapping after / .) I'll rip your goddamn head off!*
CARL. But this is all part of collaboration.
DORIAN. *(Getting the last word in.)* Like to see you try …

ALAN. *Shh!*
CARL. Just last month, for instance, we were finishing — trying to finish our Beethoven cycle in London. Let me tell you, three or four days in the studio, pretty much round the clock? Inevitably, things get tense ... *(The music shifts to onstage speakers as ...)*

Scene 8

Lights rise on a recording studio, where Elliot, Dorian and Alan listen to the playback of their latest take. A microphone is suspended in the middle of the quartet's stands. After a moment, Dorian, who has held his tongue since the preceding clash, can hold it no longer:

DORIAN. I'm sorry, I can't stand it anymore ...
ALAN. Don't.
DORIAN. This is just *bad* ...
ELLIOT. That's it, I'm leaving.
ALAN. Carl ... *(Carl joins the scene.)*
DORIAN. Fine, I'll overdub the part myself — like the Beach Boys.
CARL. Knock it off.
DORIAN. *(To an unseen engineer.)* Stop the playback! *(The music continues.)*
ELLIOT. *(To Alan.)* This was our best take.
DORIAN. We can't use it.
ALAN. Why not?
DORIAN. Don't tell me you can't hear it. Nigel! *(The music stops.)*
CARL. We can't spend the whole day on / one — *(A British-accented voice comes over the studio speakers.)*
NIGEL'S VOICE. Is there a problem?
ELLIOT. No.
CARL and ALAN. Yes.
DORIAN. *(To Nigel.)* We need to do it over.
ELLIOT. No, we don't.
ALAN. What's wrong with it?

DORIAN. For starters, the first violin's too strident.
CARL. Where?
DORIAN. Everywhere! The first fifty-three bars are marked piano.
ALAN. Plus sforzandos.
DORIAN. Yes, but —
ALAN. Hairpins …
DORIAN. *Fine,* but we don't get to *forte* until the second key change.
CARL. So?
DORIAN. So Nelly's getting piggy.
ELLIOT. "*Piggy?*"
DORIAN. Second, the B-sharps and E-sharps are too low.
ALAN. Whose?
DORIAN. Yours and Carl's.
ELLIOT. And I suppose you played flawlessly …
DORIAN. God no.
ELLIOT. Well, then.
DORIAN. I flubbed the shift into bar ten and came in a hair late at forty-seven. Also, my second double stop was off, not much, but still. *(Pause.)*
NIGEL'S VOICE. Would you like to hear it again from the top?
ALAN. Sure.
DORIAN. No.
CARL. *Dorian* …
DORIAN. I can't.
ALAN. Just to make sure.
DORIAN. I'll throw up.
ELLIOT. *It was our best take!*
CARL. That's true.
DORIAN. Which isn't good enough. *(Pause.)*
CARL. Also true. *(Pause.)*
ALAN. Well, then, we might as well make it perfect.
DORIAN. No — not perfect. Never perfect. Just closer. That's all we can hope for. *(Pause.)*
NIGEL'S VOICE. Right. Well. Why don't you all have a stretch while I set us up for take … seventeen. *(The quartet splits, Elliot and Alan one direction, Dorian and Carl the other, setting instruments aside.)*
ELLIOT. *(Sotto voce.)* God, sometimes I just want to kill him.
ALAN. He's right, though.
ELLIOT. That's *why* I want to kill him. So … *smug,* so —

CARL. Anybody hungry?
ALAN. What time is it? *(Carl checks his watch.)*
CARL. Twelve-thirty.
DORIAN. A.M. or P.M.? *(Beat. Carl checks his watch again, momentarily unsure.)*
ALAN. Let's go out and look. If the sun's up, it's lunchtime.
CARL. *(To Elliot and Dorian.)* Want anything from the machine?
ELLIOT. No. *(Dorian shakes his head. Carl and Alan exit. Elliot and Dorian wipe down their instruments in silence, each very aware of the other's presence. After a long time:)*
DORIAN. All right, maybe "piggy" was a bit much. *(Elliot continues to wipe down his violin. After a moment, Dorian sets his viola in its case.)* You never came to bed last night.
ELLIOT. I didn't feel like it.
DORIAN. That's your mantra lately. *(Elliot doesn't respond.)* I'm wearing your underwear today. Want to check?
ELLIOT. Stop it.
DORIAN. *(Approaching him.)* I'll bet you can guess which ones …
ELLIOT. Shhh!
DORIAN. Who's going to hear that hasn't known for decades? *(Elliot points to the microphone. Dorian takes the cloth from Elliot's hand and drapes it over the microphone.)* Anyway, Nigel's an old queen himself.
ELLIOT. He's got six kids.
DORIAN. Camouflage. *(Elliot betrays a smile, then settles his violin into its case. Dorian places his arms around Elliot's neck for a moment, then:)* The opening needs to be softer, that's all. Plaintive, almost a white sound, bow right over the fingerboard, like we're hearing it from a distance. *(Elliot brusquely moves away from him. Dorian continues:)* Save the vibrato for the A —
ELLIOT. Look, if you think you can play the part better —
DORIAN. You know I can. We all know. *(Beat.)* BUT, nobody asked me to be first fiddle, so *you* need to play it better. I don't mean the flashy stuff — you can still play fast, and high. And LOUD. I mean whatever's soft, or slow. Simple — from the heart. That's where you cheat. *(Elliot is stung.)* Here, I'll show you what I mean … *(Dorian picks up Elliot's violin.)*
ELLIOT. Put it down / put it down or I'll — *(He continues, overlapping.)*
DORIAN. *(Overlapping after / .)* I just want to play the —

ELLIOT. *break your fucking fingers! (Dorian stares at Elliot. Carl and Alan return with snacks.)*
ALAN. Well, it's officially night. *(Elliot snatches the violin and moves away from Dorian.)*
CARL. I'm having lunch anyway. *(He bites into a sandwich.)*
ALAN. You two should step outside, it's beautiful. The stars are … *(Turning to Carl.)* What's the word?
DORIAN. Stellar. *(He retrieves his viola.)*
CARL. *(Talking through his sandwich.)* This sandwich has got to be twenty years old.
ALAN. What's in it?
CARL. Meat.
ALAN. What kind?
CARL. The machine just said "meat."
DORIAN. Well, that narrows it down. *(Carl opens the sandwich and looks at it in a new, more skeptical light.)*
NIGEL'S VOICE. Are we ready for another take?
ALAN. One minute. *(He retrieves his bow.)*
CARL. I'm not really hungry anymore … *(He tosses the remainder aside.)*
NIGEL'S VOICE. You sound a bit muffled. Is something blocking the microphone? *(Dorian removes Elliot's cloth.)*
DORIAN. No.
NIGEL'S VOICE. That's better. This is Opus One-thirty-one, SR-51564. When you're ready. *(Alan, Dorian and Carl settle to play. Elliot, on the other hand, stands apart from them, eyes closed. Pause.)*
ALAN. El? *(After a moment, he opens his eyes.)*
ELLIOT. Not tonight. *(He quickly packs his instrument away. Carl and Alan exchange glances.)*
CARL. What do you mean "not tonight"?
ELLIOT. Exactly what I said.
ALAN. We fly home tomorrow.
ELLIOT. Then we'll have to record it at home.
CARL. We're almost done with the cycle.
ELLIOT. I'm sorry, but —
CARL. This is our last quartet!
ELLIOT. *(Abruptly.)* I've got a headache. All right? *(Beat.)*
ALAN. A *headache? (Dorian scoffs.)*
ELLIOT. *(To Dorian.) Well, you can't expect me to play from the heart when my head is pounding! (Pause.)*

NIGEL'S VOICE. Should I stop the tape? *(Elliot exits with his violin. Alan looks after him. Carl glares at Dorian. Dorian looks down.)* Gentlemen? *(Lights fade.)*

Scene 9

Music: Once more, the "Alla danza tedesca" melody, as handed off from one instrument to the next. [CD track #19.] Pin spots illuminate all four men simultaneously. Again, each is being interviewed separately.

ALAN. Our first coach was Michael Florescu.
ELLIOT. "Mihai," to be accurate.
DORIAN. More of a mentor than a coach, really.
CARL. Everybody called him "Mickey."
ELLIOT. Which he hated.
ALAN. He had a favorite saying:
ALL. *(In a thick Eastern European accent.)* "You must be like four instruments being played with one bow."
ELLIOT. Isn't that wonderful?
DORIAN. Wonderful.
ALAN. Mickey was born in Russia,
ELLIOT. He was Romanian,
ALAN. So he had this …
ELLIOT. Possibly Hungarian …
ALAN. Deep Russian soul.
CARL. Nobody knew where the hell he was from;
ELLIOT. And embodied Old World wisdom.
CARL. I don't even think he knew.
ALAN. Comic and tragic at the same time.
CARL. I mean that accent …
DORIAN. He was a genius.
ELLIOT. Charm …
CARL. Completely … *(He searches for the word.)*
ELLIOT. Elegance …
CARL. Unidentifiable.

ALAN. Like Tolstoy.
DORIAN. He would just come out with this stuff.
CARL. The quintessential European mutt.
ALAN. Wait —
DORIAN. Little pearls …
ALAN. Is that who I mean?
CARL. That accent made everything he said sound … *(He searches for the word.)*
ALAN. Who wrote *The Cherry Orchard*?
CARL. Profound.
DORIAN. Like this: *(All four speak with a thick Eastern European accent:)*
CARL. "You must
DORIAN. be like
ELLIOT. four
ALAN. instruments
CARL. being
DORIAN. played
ELLIOT. with
ALAN. one
CARL. bow."
ELLIOT. Wonderful, isn't it? *(Pause.)*
DORIAN. I think he was Czech … *(Spots out.)*

Scene 10

Music: the "Adagio ma non troppo" variation of the fourth movement of Beethoven's Opus 131. [CD track #20.] Lights rise on the quartet, playing intently in Carl's home. A child's riding toy or stuffed animal sits nearby. In the middle of the fifth bar, Alan stops playing.

ALAN. Can we not drag so much? *(The others stop.)*
ELLIOT. Who's dragging?
CARL. You.
ELLIOT. It says "adagio."

GRACE and ALAN. "Ma non troppo."
CARL. Not too much.
ELLIOT. I know what *ma non troppo* means.
ALAN. Well that was clearly troppo. It sounds like we're smothering a baby. *(Grace laughs, Alan smiles in response. Elliot notices the connection.)*
ELLIOT. All right. Bar five? *(They begin again, a bit faster. [CD track #21.])*
ALAN. *(While playing.)* Better. *(They play into bar nine. This time Carl stops.)*
CARL. Whoa whoa whoa …
ELLIOT. What now?
CARL. There's no crescendo there.
ALAN. *(Clarifying.)* Poco crescendo.
CARL. There isn't any, poco or otherwise.
ELLIOT. Well, there should be.
GRACE. Why?
ALAN. It parallels bar sixteen.
CARL. Except bar sixteen *has* a poco crescendo.
ELLIOT. So it's an echo.
CARL. An *echo?*
ALAN. Setting up bar sixteen.
CARL. Since when does an echo *precede* the sound itself?
ELLIOT. All right, if it's all about semantics …
CARL. It's not semantics, it's dynamics!
ALAN. Maybe it needs to be more poco. *(Beat.)*
ELLIOT. "More poco"?
ALAN. Little less. *(Elliot just stares at Alan in bewilderment.)*
CARL. Okay, let's not get hung up. We've got a clear choice here: We can either play it your way, or we can play it Beethoven's way.
ALAN. No no / no no no.
ELLIOT. Don't skew it like / that.
CARL. *It's in the score!*
ELLIOT. Which is open to interpretation. *(Pause.)*
CARL. If Dorian were here, he'd never let you / get away —
ALAN. Carl, don't.
ELLIOT. Yes, well, seeing as he's *not* here and the rest of us are, we'll just take a vote. Grace? *(All turn to her, a deer in the headlights.)*
GRACE. Yes?
CARL. Bar eight — with or without crescendo?

ALAN. Poco — *(Carl holds his hand up, stopping Alan. Beat.)*
GRACE. I don't want to get in the middle.
ELLIOT. You're not in the middle, it's two against one.
CARL. Shhh. *(Pause.)*
GRACE. Well, I can see both sides …
ELLIOT. Fine, Grace abstains.
ALAN. Let her finish.
GRACE. But, all other things being equal … I think we should follow what's written. *(Elliot shakes his head to himself.)*
CARL. Very wise. *(Pause.)*
ALAN. So. Two against two. *(Pause. They are at an impasse. Carl exhales heavily in exasperation.)*
CARL. Listen, I'm all for "interpretation," but if Beethoven *wanted* a crescendo in bar eight,
ALAN. *Poco* / crescendo.
CARL. he would have put one there.
ELLIOT. Not necessarily, and / maybe he did but —
CARL. What do you mean / "not necessarily," the man *(He continues, overlapping below.)*
ALAN. It might just be a misprint.
ELLIOT. How many times have we altered dynamics when we felt we needed to interpret a passage more — *(He continues, overlapping below.)*
CARL. was a perfectionist, he / marked every measure, every *note,* he didn't leave things to chance.
ALAN. Even perfectionists make mistakes, and what if the printer *wasn't* a —
CARL. *Enough. (Alan and Elliot stop talking. Beat.)* Who's got a quarter? *(He shoves a hand into his pocket.)*
ELLIOT. What are you doing?
CARL. Settling this.
ELLIOT. With a coin toss?
CARL. In three days, we've got to play this monster on national TV. We can't afford to get distracted by pointless bickering. *(Grace opens a pocket inside her viola case.)*
ELLIOT. Then why don't you stop?
CARL. *(To Grace.)* You got one?
GRACE. How about a nickel?
CARL. That'll do. *(He takes it.)* Call it in the air. *(He flips it.)*
ALAN. Heads. *(Carl catches it, slaps it on his forearm, lifts his hand,*

smiles, shows it to Elliot.)
CARL. Interpret that. *(Elliot exhales heavily in exasperation.)*
ALAN. Fine. Bar five again. *(He and Grace raise their instruments; Carl hands the nickel back to Grace, then checks his watch.)*
ELLIOT. No, I don't accept this.
ALAN. El …
ELLIOT. I don't. A coin toss is / no way —
CARL. *(Half to himself.)* Oh, shit.
ALAN. What.
CARL. *(Calling off.)* Janice! *(He stands.)*
GRACE. What is it?
CARL. I'm gonna be late. *(He sets his cello down.)*
ELLIOT. For what?
CARL. I told you I had to stop at three.
ELLIOT. No you didn't.
ALAN. Oh, right, the —
CARL. *(Exiting.) Janice!*
ELLIOT. I don't remember this.
ALAN. Yeah, he's got his appointment with the … you know, the —
GRACE. Doctor.
ALAN. Etymologist.
ELLIOT. "*Etymologist*"?
ALAN. Not etymologist, what's the —
GRACE. Entomologist.
ALAN. Right, the cancer guy. *(Beat.)*
ELLIOT. You mean "oncologist"? *(Beat.)*
ALAN. That's it. *(Beat.)*
GRACE. What's an entomologist? *(Carl reenters, pulling on a jacket.)*
CARL. Janice baked a thing, if you want some.
ALAN. Thanks.
ELLIOT. Well, there's no point rehearsing if you won't be here. *(He begins packing up his instrument.)*
CARL. Sorry, I would've canceled, but they schedule everything months in advance. *(The others start packing up. Pause. Carl removes a pacifier from his jacket pocket.)* Why is there a binky in my pocket? *(He sets it on his music stand.)*
ALAN. Hey — isn't this a big one?
CARL. Five years.
GRACE. Does that mean something?
ALAN. It means he's in the clear.

CARL. Knock wood. *(He knocks on his cello or chair.)*
ALAN. They give you something for five years?
CARL. What do you mean?
ALAN. Little trophy, box of chocolates …
CARL. I'll settle for a clean bill.
GRACE. Well, good luck.
ALAN. Yeah.
CARL. Don't say that.
ALAN. Why not?
CARL. It's bad luck. *(Beat.)*
ALAN. How is it bad luck to say "Good luck"?
CARL. It just is. It's like actors. You never say "Good luck" to an actor.
ALAN. So what do you want us to say?
CARL. *I don't care,* say whatever you want, just not "Good luck." *(He checks his watch again. Half to himself:)* Where is that woman? *(He exits again.)*
ELLIOT. I never heard about this appointment.
ALAN. Well, now you have.
ELLIOT. I thought we agreed to clear our schedules all week. I canceled *three* appointments.
ALAN. For Christ's sake, will you give him a break? He already said / he couldn't —
CARL. *(Offstage.)* I'll be in the car! *(Carl looks in.)* See you tomorrow. *(He starts out again.)*
ALAN. Carl.
CARL. *(Turning back.)* Huh? *(Beat.)*
ALAN. Break a leg. *(Beat.)*
GRACE. Yeah, break a leg. *(Beat.)*
CARL. Yeah. Thanks. *(He exits. Elliot finishes packing up and stands with his case.)*
ELLIOT. *(To Grace.)* Insects.
GRACE. What?
ELLIOT. Entomologists study insects.
GRACE. Oh. Right. Thanks. *(Elliot exits. She looks at Alan. Lights fade.)*

Scene 11

In darkness, a poignant ballad with the popular California sound of the sixties begins to play. [Not included on CD.] After a few moments, a loud buzzer is heard; the music continues. Again, the buzzer, more insistent; the music continues. Finally, the buzzer sounds over and over. Lights up on Dorian's apartment. A few packing boxes are on the floor, a boom box (now the source of the music) sits atop a chair. Elliot's open violin case rests nearby. Elliot has just entered; Dorian holds a short plunger.

DORIAN. Nelly! Perfect timing!
ELLIOT. Where is it?
DORIAN. I was just about to unclog my toilet …
ELLIOT. Knock it off.
DORIAN. Got me thinking of you. And listen: *(Indicating the boom box.)* They're playing our s — *(Elliot pushes him hard, knocking him backward into the room. Dorian recovers his balance.)* Well, that's the most physical we've gotten in months.
ELLIOT. You've crossed a line.
DORIAN. I take it you got my note.
ELLIOT. I almost called the police, you know that?
DORIAN. What would you tell them? "My lover — oops, *coworker* — kidnapped my violin?" Sounds a little squishy. *(A brief standoff. Then Elliot walks past Dorian and exits into an offstage room.)* Sorry for the mess in the bedroom. I haven't had a chance to unpack everything. Anything, really. Oh, I got some of your clothes by mistake. Good thing you sewed name tags in them. *(Elliot reenters and crosses to another interior exit. Before he disappears:)* It's not in the kitchen. *(Sounds of pans clattering, cabinets shutting. Dorian starts flipping the plunger, catching it by the handle.)* You haven't told me what you think of the new place. Not as nice as ours, of course. BUT, older buildings have their charms: clawfoot tubs, cast-iron radiators … Nice wide window ledges for those too timid to face a bare bodkin. *(Elliot reenters.)* I told you it wasn't in the kitchen.

ELLIOT. You think this is some kind of *joke?*
DORIAN. I wanted to see you.
ELLIOT. You see me every day.
DORIAN. Outside of rehearsal.
ELLIOT. Well, here I am. Happy?
DORIAN. God no.
ELLIOT. I step out for a bite. I come home to practice the Brahms and find a *ransom note (He pulls a note out of his shirt pocket, printed words taped to it like a ransom note.)* taped to my music stand.
DORIAN. I thought you'd appreciate the fact that I cut the words out of *Chamber Music Monthly.*
ELLIOT. You've crossed a line. I don't know who you are.
DORIAN. The feeling's mutual. *(Beat.)* You treat me like an employee, won't even make eye contact anymore. Bad enough that our playing suffers …
ELLIOT. Have you been taking your meds?
DORIAN. Ah, here we go …
ELLIOT. I'm just asking.
DORIAN. Blame it on the crazy one …
ELLIOT. I never said —
DORIAN. I flushed them down the toilet. All of them. *(Beat.)*
ELLIOT. You shouldn't have done that.
DORIAN. So I discovered. *(He holds up the plunger.)* At the very least, I should have taken them out of the bottles. I was about to pour Drano down, but I thought it might react with the lithium. *(Elliot shakes his head and walks away. Pause.)* They flatten me out, make me feel dead. Make it so I can't hear the music / anymore.
ELLIOT. *I don't care,* just tell me where it is! *(Pause. Sensing Elliot's intransigence, Dorian jams the plunger onto the seat of the chair, making it stick, then exits into the bedroom. Elliot removes the plunger and places the open case upon the chair. Dorian reenters carrying the violin. Elliot takes it quickly and looks it over. As he places it in its case:)*
DORIAN. It was under my pillow. You know how I hate to sleep alone. *(Elliot closes the case.)*
ELLIOT. The others are going to hear about this. *(He heads toward the exit.)*
DORIAN. You don't have to go so soon, you know. *(Elliot wheels around.)*
ELLIOT. What did you expect me to do?
DORIAN. When?

ELLIOT. Tonight!
DORIAN. I don't know. I thought you might like to play duets. It's been a while. *(Elliot looks away.)* I don't mind your being testy. Even furious. At least it's something. What I can't take is cold. Icy, cold, *objective* ...
ELLIOT. Yes, well. Someone's got to maintain a grip on reality. *(Dorian lowers his head. Elliot studies him for a moment.)* Give me the key.
DORIAN. Key?
ELLIOT. To my apartment.
DORIAN. *Our* apart/ment.
ELLIOT. There is no "our" apartment; not anymore. *(Dorian reluctantly produces a key, which Elliot pockets. He starts out, then stops, turns back.)* And stay away from the ledges. *(He exits. Lights fade.)*

Scene 12

Music: the "Prelude" of Bach's G Major Suite for Unaccompanied Cello, transcribed for viola. [CD track #22.] A pin spot rises on Grace, sitting by a music stand, viola in hand. Music fades out.

GRACE. Well, they came to my school, I guess I was ... nine, nine or ten. I don't remember what they — No, that's not true. I remember they ended with a Beach Boys song, transcribed for string quartet. I guess they thought it would make it look cool, you know, to study a stringed instrument. But nobody my age even knew who the Beach Boys were.

Anyway, after the assembly, Mr. Stritch asked me if I thought I might like to learn to play something, and I said, "I want the big violin." I didn't even know what it was called, I just — There was something about that ... dark, chocolate sound — it was a little butch or something, I don't know what it was, I just *wanted* it, I wanted to make that sound.

So Mr. Stritch let me sign one out to take home and show my parents, and my father ... *(She pauses, confronting the memory.)* It was like I'd brought home a stray *dog* or something — you know, a muddy old, half-blind, three-legged mutt that farted. He just didn't get it. I told them, "It's called a viola, and I'm gonna learn how to play it." And Mom said, "That's nice, honey — as long as you get all your homework done." But Daddy just stood there, staring at it. As if it were something smelly that would someday shit in his shoes. *(Sometime during the preceding, a man has entered behind Grace, and lights have risen slowly to reveal Elliot, violin case and music in hand.)* Anyway, now that I'm *in* the quartet —

ELLIOT. Knock / knock.

GRACE. *(Startled.) Oh!*

ELLIOT. Sorry.

GRACE. Oh my —

ELLIOT. I didn't mean to frighten you.

GRACE. How did / you —

ELLIOT. Your door was open.

GRACE. No it isn't.

ELLIOT. Unlocked. I rang the bell …

GRACE. It's broken. *(Beat.)*

ELLIOT. Well, then, that would explain why you didn't answer. *(Grace tries to recompose herself as Elliot sets his case and music down. He sniffles.)* What were you doing?

GRACE. What do you mean?

ELLIOT. When I came in.

GRACE. Oh — you know. Warming up.

ELLIOT. Sounded like you were practicing a speech.

GRACE. Oh, no, just talking to myself. Only Child Syndrome. Nobody my own age to fight with. *(Elliot nods vaguely, unconvinced. He sits, opens his case, then rests his head in his hand, shutting his eyes. Grace takes this in.)* Everything all right?

ELLIOT. Hmm? Yes. Perfect. I just haven't been sleeping well. For a while now.

GRACE. Do you want something to drink?

ELLIOT. No, thanks.

GRACE. I've got coffee — well, instant …

ELLIOT. Just a cup of hot water.

GRACE. Water?

ELLIOT. Hot. Preferably scalding. *(Beat.)*

GRACE. Okay … *(She exits. From offstage:)* I know Alan drinks coffee, so I bought — *(Elliot sneezes.)* What?

ELLIOT. Nothing. *(Elliot removes a handkerchief and wipes his nose.)*
GRACE. *(Offstage.)* Anyway, I hope he doesn't mind instant.
ELLIOT. You wouldn't happen to have a cat, would you?
GRACE. *(Offstage.)* Three.
ELLIOT. *(Sotto voce.)* Christ …
GRACE. *(Offstage.)* I hope you're not allergic …
ELLIOT. Well, it's a little late to ask now, isn't it? *(She reenters with a large mug of water.)*
GRACE. I'm sorry, I didn't —
ELLIOT. No reason you should have. Is that mine?
GRACE. Yeah. *(She hands him the cup.)* I never heard of anybody drinking hot — *(Elliot immerses his left hand in the hot water, wincing slightly.)* Oh!
ELLIOT. I got into thc habit at Curtis. A necessary prologue for cold winter mornings when we'd start practicing at six or seven. Anything to thaw the blood. *(He smiles. Beat.)*
GRACE. I'm *really* loving this quartet, by the way.
ELLIOT. The Beethoven or the foursome?
GRACE. Oh — well … both. I mean, I meant the music, but … both. *(Beat.)*
ELLIOT. How would you like to record it?
GRACE. Yes! Of coursc.
ELLIOT. It would complete our Beethoven cycle. We … hit a snag a few years ago and never finished it.
GRACE. So I heard. *(Beat.)*
ELLIOT. "Heard"? *(Beat.)*
GRACE. Somewhere. I don't remember. *(Elliot nods slightly, looking at her all the while. After a moment, he takes his hand out of the mug and dries it with a rag from his case.)*
ELLIOT. Our work is ephemeral. Like us. The notes pass by, then disappear forever. That's why a resonant hall is so poignant: The sound lasts a half-second longer, giving the brief illusion of immortality. *(He sets down the rag and lifts his violin from its case.)* A Beethoven cycle, though, well, that might feel like an *opus,* something … worthy of posterity.
GRACE. Your other recordings will last. *(He scoffs.)*
ELLIOT. Half are already out of print.
GRACE. At least the Bartóks.
ELLIOT. Maybe, for a while. Since it won the Grammy. But even that will wind up in the remainder bin, like Peter Frampton.

GRACE. Who? *(Beat.)*
ELLIOT. My point exactly. *(Alan is heard approaching:)*
ALAN. *(Offstage.)* What a game what a game what a *game. (He has entered.)* Did you finish it?
GRACE. No. *(Alan lets out a cry of disbelief.)* I was tired!
ALAN. When did you turn it off?
GRACE. Soon as you left.
ALAN. Bottom of the fifth?
GRACE. I don't remember.
ELLIOT. *(Wiping his nose.)* What game?
ALAN. *Game six,* what do you — Never mind. *(To Grace.)* You missed a helluva comeback. *(To Elliot.)* What did you do last night?
ELLIOT. I practiced.
ALAN. Oh, that. *(He begins unpacking his violin.)*
ELLIOT. You would have done well to do the same.
ALAN. I practiced in grad school. *(He glances at Grace, who smiles, then attaches his shoulder rest.)*
GRACE. You want some coffee?
ALAN. Great.
GRACE. *(Starting off.)* It's instant.
ALAN. Uh, never mind then.
GRACE. Oh — sorry.
ALAN. That's okay.
GRACE. I don't have a coffee maker.
ALAN. It's fine — I caffeinated at home. *(She sits. Alan retrieves his bow, perhaps begins rosining it. He considers Elliot for a few moments before speaking.)* So, El. I wanted you to know, I filed a report. *(Elliot just looks at him. Beat.)*
GRACE. Report?
ALAN. *(To Grace.)* Missing Persons.
ELLIOT. Why did you do that?
ALAN. Nobody's seen him in weeks.
ELLIOT. Maybe that's the way he wants it.
ALAN. I talked to his landlady. She opened up his apartment. There was no sign of anybody living there — all his plants were dead …
ELLIOT. They're always dead.
ALAN. Still —
ELLIOT. He *buys* them dead.
ALAN. *I got worried,* that's all.

ELLIOT. You don't think I'm worried?
ALAN. I didn't / say that.
ELLIOT. If anyone should tell the police, it's me.
ALAN. Well, you didn't, so I did.
ELLIOT. Did you at least call his mother?
ALAN. He hates his mother, they haven't talked / in —
ELLIOT. If you file a report, they're going to try to reach her. You want her to find out from Officer Krupke? *(Beat.)*
ALAN. All right, I'll call her, can you give me her number?
ELLIOT. I have it at home. She's upstate somewhere.
ALAN. *(To Grace.)* I'll call collect. *(She smiles. Carl enters wearing a Yankees cap and lugging his cello.)*
CARL. Did you see the game?
ALAN. *(The question's absurd.)* Did I see the game …
CARL. *(To Grace.)* You?
GRACE. Some.
ELLIOT. *What game?*
CARL. American League Championship.
ALAN. How about that double play at the plate?
CARL. Oh my god …
ALAN. Like nothin'.
CARL. Business as usual.
ALAN. And some people think he's overpaid.
CARL. Underpaid, you ask me.
ELLIOT. This was a baseball game? *(They all stare at him. Beat.)*
ALAN. Yeah, the national pastime. *(Carl chuckles, begins unpacking his cello.)*
GRACE. *(To Carl.)* How was your check-up? *(Carl continues, as if he hasn't heard the question.)*
ALAN. Carl?
CARL. Huh?
GRACE. Everything go okay?
CARL. Yeah, fine.
GRACE. Great.
ALAN. So, clean bill, huh? *(Carl sits.)*
CARL. What's today, second movement?
GRACE. Um … yeah.
ALAN. They did give you the all-clear, didn't they?
CARL. Let's just play. *(Pause.)*
ELLIOT. Right. The "Allegro molto vivace." *(All find the appropri-*

ate page. Elliot cues, they begin playing. [CD track #23.] The poco ritardando *in bar eight is sloppy. Carl stops.)*
CARL. Not together. *(The others stop.)*
ELLIOT. I've got the moving part, listen to me.
ALAN. We need a signal.
ELLIOT. No you don't, just listen to the eighths.
CARL. All right. Again? *(They play. [CD track #24.] This time bar eight sounds together, but Elliot stops playing in bar ten.)*
ELLIOT. *(To Alan.)* That's in tempo.
ALAN. So?
CARL. He means it should be and it wasn't.
ALAN. Where?
GRACE. After the poco ritard.
ALAN. I played in tempo.
ELLIOT. No you didn't.
CARL. Try it again.
ALAN. I know I did.
ELLIOT. It was sluggish.
CARL. *Last time.* Top of the page. *(They play. [CD track #25.] Around bar ten, they begin to speak while playing:)*
ELLIOT. That's it.
CARL. Go on. *(They continue playing.)*
ALAN. Watch the hairpins …
ELLIOT. Who?
ALAN. You. *(Elliot stops playing; the others follow.)*
ELLIOT. I'm playing the hairpins.
ALAN. That's the problem — you're putting them in where they don't belong.
ELLIOT. Maybe you're missing some.
ALAN. No, look — it's one long build till bar seventeen.
ELLIOT. Which is what I played.
GRACE. No you didn't. *(Elliot looks at her. Beat.)* I heard it too. *(Beat. Elliot sniffles.)*
CARL. Well, then let's take it back.
ALAN. The in tempo. *(They play from bar nine. [CD track #26.] After bar seventeen:)* Better. *(They continue through bar twenty-six, where Elliot explodes:)*
ELLIOT. *Must* you keep doing that? *(They stop.)*
ALAN. What?
ELLIOT. Ogling her.

ALAN. I'm not og — I was making eye contact.
ELLIOT. Well, stop it.
GRACE. We come in at the same / time.
ELLIOT. If you want to play together, then watch the fingers — that's where the notes are, here, not *here.* If you want to play footsie, make "eye contact."
ALAN. I wasn't —
CARL. Just drop it.
ALAN. He's the one who won't —
CARL. Everybody drop it. From the beginning …
ELLIOT. Also, you're flat.
ALAN. Who?
ELLIOT. Grace.
GRACE. I don't think so.
ELLIOT. I'm not talking about your tits, I'm / talking *(He continues, overlapping.)*
CARL. *(A warning.)* Hey.
ELLIOT. *(Continuing.)* about your D string.
ALAN. What the hell is wrong with you?
ELLIOT. *(To Alan.)* You think I don't know what's going on?
CARL. *(To Elliot.)* You need to chill out.
ELLIOT. *(To Carl.)* We had an agreement.
CARL. I don't know what / you're —
ELLIOT. "No romantic entanglements in the quartet."
ALAN. You should talk.
ELLIOT. Exactly — now we know it doesn't work.
CARL. Who's having a / romantic —
ALAN. Nobody.
ELLIOT. What were you doing here last night?
ALAN. We had dinner!
ELLIOT. What else?
CARL. Stop.
ALAN. We watched the game!
ELLIOT. And?
CARL. *Stop it now.*
ALAN. What are you trying to prove?
ELLIOT. *I know you I know your libido and / I say it's not going to happen.*
CARL. Elliot, for Christ's sake, *shut the fuck up! (Pause.)*
ELLIOT. Fine, I'll shut up. *(He stands and begins packing his vio-*

lin away. Long pause. Then:)
GRACE. *(To others; helpfully.)* If you want, we can take our break now. *(She checks her watch.)*
ALAN. El … *(Elliot sneezes.)*
GRACE. I mean, I know it's early … *(Elliot puts on his jacket.)*
CARL. Where are you going? *(Elliot walks out. Grace calls after him:)*
GRACE. I made muffins … *(A door slams offstage. Pause. Carl and Alan exchange glances.)* This is my fault …
CARL. No.
GRACE. It is.
ALAN. This has nothing / to do —
GRACE. *The cats.*
CARL. What?
GRACE. I should've told him about the cats.
ALAN. It's not about the cats.
GRACE. He's really allergic, / he started —
CARL. *It's not the cats. (Pause.)*
GRACE. Should I go after him?
ALAN. He'll be back. He left the violin. *(Silence.)*
GRACE. This is falling apart, isn't it? *(Pause.)*
ALAN. *(Unconvincingly.)* No.
GRACE. Oh, God. I should've known.
CARL. He'll be back. *(Long pause.)*
GRACE. I'm going to go after him. *(She exits. Pause. Alan exhales heavily.)*
ALAN. Seems like old times, doesn't it?
CARL. Don't get me started. *(Long pause.)*
ALAN. So. How was it really?
CARL. Huh?
ALAN. Your five-year…?
CARL. Oh. Good.
ALAN. Really?
CARL. I mean, you never know. They always find something to fuss about …
ALAN. Right.
CARL. "Ooh, your liver enzymes are elevated … " *(Beat.)*
ALAN. What's that mean?
CARL. Who the hell knows? It means now they can charge for a PET scan and make even more money.
ALAN. Goddamn doctors.

CARL. BUT — so far, so good. *(He knocks on his cello.)*
ALAN. Great. *(Silence.)*
CARL. Are you balling Grace?
ALAN. No.
CARL. Really?
ALAN. Yeah. No.
CARL. Good. 'Cause that'll muck things up. *(Pause.)*
ALAN. We just had dinner, that's all.
CARL. Dinner's fine. *(Pause.)*
ALAN. I mean, even if things *were* to get serious —
CARL. They won't. *(Beat.)*
ALAN. No?
CARL. No. *(Pause.)*
ALAN. Why won't they?
CARL. Because I'd cut your dick off. *(Beat.)*
ALAN. Oh. Okay.
CARL. Just so you know.
ALAN. Right. *(They sit in silence. Lights fade.)*

Scene 13

In darkness, the sound of various violas practicing the orchestral excerpts from Richard Strauss' Don Juan. *[Optional. CD track #27.] Gradually, the more distant violas fade, leaving a single instrument playing. [CD track #28.] A blistering passage ends on a high note that is slightly flat. Lights up on Grace, who stands with her instrument before a folding music stand. Frustrated with her high note, she prepares to launch in again. Dorian stands a few yards behind her. Before she can resume playing:*

DORIAN. Don't hold back. *(Grace turns around, startled.)* That's why you're missing the high D — you don't expect to make it, so you fall short. But there's no reason, you've got the notes. You're just afraid to go all the way. *(Beat.)* Anyway, my two cents.
GRACE. Well … thanks. *(Grace turns away to begin practicing*

again. Dorian interrupts:)
DORIAN. Do you know who I am? *(She stops, but doesn't turn around.)* I know who you are. And yet we've never met, that's strange, don't you think, I do. I think that's *very* strange. *(She turns around to face him.)* Then again, *I'm* strange, so you never know.
GRACE. I'm sorry, I … need to warm up. *(She turns away.)*
DORIAN. No, you don't. You're just scared of me. *(Beat. She turns toward him.)*
GRACE. No, I'm not. *(Beat.)*
DORIAN. Good. *(Pause. A voice calls from offstage:)*
VOICE. *(Offstage.)* Number fifty-one.
DORIAN. It's wonderful, isn't it?
GRACE. What?
DORIAN. The Lazara.
GRACE. Oh.
DORIAN. Lower strings rich and resonant, but with absolute clarity, not too nasal on the A …
GRACE. It's a beautiful instrument.
DORIAN. Can I hold it? *(She doesn't respond.)* Please. *(She hesitates.)* I'm not buggy anymore, if that's what you're thinking. *(She hesitates a moment longer, then hands him the instrument. Dorian takes it, looks it over, smells it with pleasure, then places it under his chin.)* God — it feels huge.
GRACE. It's not even sixteen and a half.
DORIAN. I know, but I've only played violin lately, so to me it's gargantuan. *(He shuts his eyes and moves his right arm as if bowing.)* Ah, that's it — smooth and creamy on the bottom … *(He "plays" some more. Grace looks around, self-conscious.)* And up on top … *(He "plays" onto the higher strings.)*
GRACE. Um …
DORIAN. Cuts through without being crass — bold, not brazen.
GRACE. I'd like it back now. *(Beat.)*
DORIAN. Of course. *(He hands over the viola, letting his fingers linger on the body of the viola as it changes hands.)* Did they tell you I was buggy?
GRACE. No.
DORIAN. *No?*
GRACE. Well, yes, actually, they did.
DORIAN. I should hope so; I was in a bad way, pharmaceutically speaking. But now I'm on a very good regimen: Prozac and Xanax

and Valproic acid. Which, I'm discovering, makes me sound like Julie Andrews: *(Singing, to the tune of "My Favorite Things":)* "Prozac and Xanax and Valproic acid … " *(Grace smiles.)* There's a smile. *(Now self-conscious, she drops it.)* I'm surprised to find you in Pittsburgh, a day before your big concert.
GRACE. We're rehearsing tonight.
DORIAN. Do the others know you're here? *(Beat.)* I didn't think so.
GRACE. You're auditioning, too?
DORIAN. Yes, well, I can't live off Mother's largesse forever. Or my severance package. Which was nothing. "Please be advised that your employment with the Lazara Quartet is hereby terminated." No gold watch. So — drag out the orchestral excerpts: *Don Juan, Bartered Bride, Roumanian Rhapsody* …
GRACE. What's your number?
DORIAN. I'm next. *(Beat.)*
GRACE. Shouldn't you be warming up?
DORIAN. *(Indicating her viola.)* I just did. *(He smiles.)* What are you playing at the White House?
GRACE. Beethoven.
DORIAN. Early? Middle?
GRACE. One-thirty-one. *(Beat.)*
DORIAN. Really. *(She nods. He considers this. Then:)* Don't let Elliot get too strident. It'll spoil it.
GRACE. Okay. *(Beat.)*
DORIAN. Has he been a prick to you yet?
GRACE. Once or twice. *(They share a smile.)*
DORIAN. Well, don't take it personally. You're sitting in the scapegoat seat.
VOICE. *(Offstage.)* Number fifty-two.
GRACE. Is that you?
DORIAN. Hmm?
GRACE. Number fifty-two?
DORIAN. Ah. Yes.
GRACE. Good luck. *(She turns away.)*
DORIAN. Um …
GRACE. *(Turning back.)* Yes?
DORIAN. This may seem a little awkward …
GRACE. What's that?
VOICE. *(Offstage.)* Fifty-two?
DORIAN. *(Calling off.)* Just a moment, please. *(To Grace.)* Can I

use the Lazara? *(Beat.)* If you don't mind. The viola I borrowed doesn't know the notes. *(Beat.)*
GRACE. I'm —
DORIAN. I'll give it back as soon as I'm done, I promise. In one piece. *(She hesitates for a moment, then hands it over.)* I'll need your bow, too. *(She looks at it, then gives it to him.)* Thank you. *(He disappears off as she looks after him, then returns a few seconds later.)* Remember: Don't hold back. *(He exits again. Lights fade.)*

Scene 14

Music: a sprightly string quartet arrangement of "Hail to the Chief." [CD track #29.] When it is finished, lights up on a backstage room at the White House. Elliot and Alan quarrel as Carl sits working on a crossword puzzle. All are elegantly dressed in formal wear. Elliot soaks his left hand in a mug of water with the presidential seal.

ELLIOT. They're too bright.
ALAN. I told her.
ELLIOT. Told who?
ALAN. Marcia.
ELLIOT. Who the hell is Marcia?
ALAN. The *girl,* the … assistant to the —
ELLIOT. *Oh,* the one you've been flirting with all night.
ALAN. I wasn't flirting!
ELLIOT. So what is Marcia going to do about it?
ALAN. Nothing. *(Beat.)*
ELLIOT. Why not?
ALAN. They set them this afternoon.
ELLIOT. But they're too bright.
ALAN. I know.
ELLIOT. So they should change them.
ALAN. They can't.
ELLIOT. Of course they can — if they can set them, they / can —
ALAN. They're for the TV cameras.

ELLIOT. Oh for god's sake …
ALAN. You want to be seen by fifteen million people?
ELLIOT. Yes! But if I can't read the notes on the page —
ALAN. You know the notes.
ELLIOT. That's beside the point. Carl …
ALAN. Look, we spent an hour and a half checking levels this afternoon.
ELLIOT. They were fine then.
ALAN. They're fine now, they haven't changed.
ELLIOT. Did you even ask her whether they could be lowered?
ALAN. No, El, I didn't. *(Beat.)*
ELLIOT. Why not?
ALAN. Because they're *fine.*
ELLIOT. They're blinding!
ALAN. They're the levels we agreed on. Carl?
CARL. *(Not looking up.)* Leave me out of it.
ELLIOT. I can't play my best / if —
ALAN. You do this every time: "The lights are too bright," "The lights are too *dim,*" "The stage is too *hot,*" "The chairs are too *low*" …
ELLIOT. If I'm not comfortable —
ALAN. *You're never comfortable!* Never! But it has nothing to do with the lights or the chairs or the pollen count. It's just you, El. *(Pause.)*
ELLIOT. *(To Carl.)* You didn't think the lights were too bright?
CARL. They never gave us dessert … *(Carl checks his watch.)*
ALAN. I think they're serving it now. *(Carl tosses down the crossword puzzle.)*
CARL. Anybody want some? *(He stands.)*
ELLIOT. We go on in ten minutes …
CARL. Then I've got ten minutes. Where's Grace?
ALAN. Down the hall.
ELLIOT. Not throwing up in the China Room…?
CARL. Huh? *(Elliot waves off the joke.)*
ALAN. She's warming up. *(Carl nods and exits. Elliot sets down the mug and dries his hand on a cloth. Alan looks after Carl. When he's sure Carl is out of earshot:)* El? *(Elliot does not respond.)* Elliot.
ELLIOT. What.
ALAN. Janice called me last night. *(Elliot turns to face him.)*
ELLIOT. Janice?
ALAN. While Carl was out of the house. *(Elliot remains silent.)*

She was sobbing. Soon as I picked up, she just lost it. *(Pause.)*
ELLIOT. It's back?
ALAN. It's in his brain, his liver …
ELLIOT. Oh, Christ …
ALAN. She was afraid he might not tell us, you know Carl, "keep it together … "
ELLIOT. *(Still reeling.)* God*damn* …
ALAN. But she said he took it pretty hard.
ELLIOT. Have you said anything?
ALAN. Not to him. *(Pause. Elliot exhales heavily.)*
ELLIOT. I knew this was going to happen; something had to happen to … *intrude,* now, just when we're finding our balance, starting to think about the — *(He stops short. Alan turns to see why. Carl has just entered with a plate of cheesecake; he now notes the halt in conversation. Pause.)*
CARL. Five minutes.
ELLIOT. Thank you.
ALAN. Thanks. *(Elliot and Alan busy themselves.)*
ELLIOT. What's that, cheesecake?
CARL. More or less. *(He sits, eats. Pause.)*
ALAN. I ought to find Grace … *(He starts out.)*
CARL. She's in the ladies'. *(Alan returns. Carl watches him carefully. Pause.)*
ALAN. Ironic how even in the White House they still relegate the artists to the room beside the kitchen.
ELLIOT. Especially in the White House. *(Pause.)*
ALAN. *(Of the cheesecake.)* That any good?
CARL. *(To Alan.)* She called you, didn't she. *(Beat. Elliot turns to face him.)*
ALAN. Yeah.
CARL. Woman never could keep a secret … *(He takes a bite.)*
ALAN. She needed to talk to somebody, figured you did, too … *(Carl nods.)* I'm sorry, Carl. God, it's shitty luck.
CARL. Yeah. *(Pause.)*
ALAN. Anything you need, you know …
ELLIOT. Absolutely.
ALAN. Just ask.
CARL. Explain it to my kids? *(Elliot looks at Alan. Beat.)*
ALAN. Explain it?
CARL. 'Cause I'm — I don't see how I'm gonna do it. And Janice,

well, you know, she'll just … *(Pause.)* Last time, Kara was too young to know what was going on, Tim wasn't even born. Now they're both gonna wonder why Daddy's losing his hair, and his lunch, and his sense of humor. What am I supposed to tell them? *(Beat.)*
ELLIOT. Tell them the truth. *(Carl scoffs.)*
CARL. Not a chance. *(Pause. He holds out his plate.)* Want some cheesecake? *(Elliot passes.)*
ALAN. Yeah, sure. *(He takes it.)* How is it?
CARL. Not New York. But what are you gonna do? *(Alan takes a bite. Grace enters with her viola, wearing an exquisite and flattering gown.)*
GRACE. We're on.
ELLIOT. Now?
GRACE. She just called places.
ELLIOT. Gentlemen, man your battle stations. *(They retrieve their instruments.)*
ALAN. *(To Grace.)* Did I tell you you look wonderful tonight?
CARL. *(Before Grace can respond.)* No, and you're not going to.
ELLIOT. They're opening the door.
ALAN. Let's go. *(Alan and Elliot exit. Carl rests his head momentarily against the scroll of his cello. A man is faintly heard speaking on a microphone in the distance:)*
PRESIDENT. *(Offstage.)* … And so, Mr. Chairman, it is my honor and pleasure tonight to introduce to you one of America's cultural treasures …
GRACE. *(To Carl.)* Are you okay? *(Carl looks up.)*
PRESIDENT. Musical ambassadors to the world …
CARL. Play every note.
PRESIDENT. *(Offstage.)* The Lazara String Quartet. *(Applause. They exit as lights fade.)*

Scene 15

In darkness, as the applause fades, music fades up: the finale of Beethoven's Opus 131. [CD track #30.] After the final notes have died, applause fills the void, interspersed with an occasional "Bravo!" Lights rise on the backstage room as the quartet enters. The applause continues offstage.

CARL. That'll do.
ALAN. Hot damn!
ELLIOT. Listen to that. *(They listen for a few seconds.)*
GRACE. Oh my —
ELLIOT. Listen. *(The applause continues for a few seconds.)*
ALAN. Wow.
CARL. I'd say they liked it. *(They listen for a few seconds.)*
ELLIOT. Let's take another bow.
ALAN. She said not to.
CARL. Who.
ALAN. Marcia.
CARL. Who?
ELLIOT. The chickie with the cleavage.
CARL. Oh, screw her.
ELLIOT. Take another bow.
ALAN. But —
CARL and ELLIOT. Go! *(They push him off, then follow with Grace. Applause increases for a few moments, then the quartet reenters.)*
ELLIOT. They're going to want an encore.
GRACE. Encore?
ALAN. We can't.
CARL. *(To Elliot.)* How about the fugue from / Opus —
ELLIOT. Opus Fifty-nine, Number Three, good.
ALAN. There isn't time —
GRACE. I don't know the fugue.
ELLIOT. I've got the parts in my case. *(He starts for his case.)*
GRACE. But —
CARL. Wait. *(They stop, listen.)* It's stopping. *(Sure enough, the*

applause is diminishing. Elliot looks off.)
ELLIOT. They're closing the door. *(The remaining applause cuts off. Pause.)*
ALAN. Right.
CARL. Fine.
ELLIOT. Another day, then.
GRACE. Another day. *(They begin wiping down and packing up their instruments, still aglow. After a few moments:)*
CARL. Did anybody look at the president during the Fourth Variation?
ALAN. Don't tell me he was yawning …
CARL. Crying.
ALAN. Get out.
GRACE. Really?
ELLIOT. I thought he was removing his contacts.
ALAN. I'd like to believe the man has a heart, despite his track record.
ELLIOT. Gentlemen, may I suggest we record Opus One-thirty-one as soon as possible? I have a feeling our Beethoven cycle is going to be much in — *(Elliot stops dead upon seeing Dorian, who has entered wearing formal attire. Beat.)*
DORIAN. *(To Elliot.)* Bravo. *(Grace turns.)* Brava.
ALAN. Dorian …
DORIAN. Quite, quite beautiful.
GRACE. Thank you.
DORIAN. *(To Alan.)* And, by the way, he was crying.
ELLIOT. What are you doing here?
DORIAN. Mother was invited. *(He removes an invitation from his pocket as proof.)* Apparently giving buckets of money to the party buys you dinner and a show. *(He pockets the invitation again.)* Also, my tux was tired of being in the closet. And we know how vexing that can be, don't we, Nelly?
ALAN. Where the hell have you been?
DORIAN. Upstate.
ELLIOT. *Upstate?*
ALAN. I didn't know if you were dead or alive.
ELLIOT. You hate your mother …
DORIAN. So I discovered. BUT — any port in a storm. Anyway, I only stopped by to offer my congratulations.
CARL. Thank you.

ALAN. Thanks, Dor.
DORIAN. You're welcome. *(To Grace.)* And double congratulations to you. *(Beat. Carl and Alan exchange glances.)*
ELLIOT. Why double congratulations to her?
DORIAN. Didn't she tell you?
ALAN. Tell us what?
DORIAN. About her phone call.
ELLIOT. Phone call?
DORIAN. *(To Grace.)* I guess not.
CARL. What phone call?
DORIAN. From Pittsburgh. *(Beat.)*
GRACE. *(Bitterly.)* You didn't have to do that.
ELLIOT. You took the audition?
GRACE. I wasn't sure you needed to know.
DORIAN. They've asked her to be their principal / violist.
ALAN. *(Overlapping after /.)* Oh, Christ …
GRACE. *(To Carl.)* I haven't accepted yet.
ELLIOT. You took the fucking audition …
GRACE. *(To Dorian.) And I really don't appreciate you telling them for me.*
ALAN. *(To Dorian.)* How did you find out?
DORIAN. They offered me the job first.
ELLIOT. You should have taken it.
DORIAN. No, I realized I'd rather play string quartets.
ELLIOT. Good luck finding one who'd take you.
DORIAN. I think I already have. *(He looks at Carl.)*
CARL. Don't.
DORIAN. At least, I'm hoping so.
CARL. Not here.
ELLIOT. *(To Carl.)* What's he talking about?
DORIAN. I called Carl last night …
ALAN. *(To Dorian.)* Carl?
DORIAN. Invited him over and made a proposal.
CARL. Damn it, I told you, this / wasn't —
ELLIOT. No.
ALAN. *(To Dorian.)* Why didn't you call me, / I've been —
ELLIOT. No, I know where this is going …
DORIAN. You don't.
ELLIOT. He wants back in, and I won't let him.
CARL. Elliot …

ELLIOT. No! I'd take Richard first, or the guy with the hair. Besides, Grace hasn't said yes to Pittsburgh. *(To Grace.)* You haven't, have you.
GRACE. No.
ELLIOT. Good; don't.
GRACE. But I need to give them an / answer —
ELLIOT. What did you just experience out there? What did that feel like? To have Beethoven flowing through you, through all four of us, like an electric current. You think you're going to find that playing boom-chick boom-chick?
ALAN. Let her make her own decision.
ELLIOT. You *want* her to take it?
ALAN. *No,* but —
ELLIOT. You want to go back to the way things were before we found her?
DORIAN. Actually, that wasn't my proposal. *(Elliot and Alan look at Dorian. Beat.)*
ALAN. It wasn't?
CARL. *(To Dorian.)* I told you to wait, I specifically said —
DORIAN. *I couldn't wait.* And neither can you.
ELLIOT. What's his proposal? *(Pause.)*
CARL. Dorian was hoping that Grace would stay with the quartet.
GRACE. Stay?
ELLIOT. And what would you get out of that?
DORIAN. That depends on what the rest of you decide. *(He looks at Alan.)*
ALAN. Wait — you don't mean…? *(Dorian nods.)*
ELLIOT. *(To Carl.)* What's going on? *(Beat.)*
CARL. He wants to replace you, Elliot. *(Elliot takes this in for a moment, then looks at Dorian, then Alan, then back at Carl. He starts to chuckle in disbelief.)*
ELLIOT. Well, tell him he can't.
CARL. I'm not sure I want to.
ALAN. Carl …
ELLIOT. *Of course you want to,* it's a ridiculous notion!
CARL. So I thought at first.
ALAN. Hold on …
ELLIOT. This is the man whose tantrums wasted hours of precious rehearsal time, whose … obstinacy turned recording sessions / into grueling —

ALAN. Look, maybe this isn't the / time or —
ELLIOT. *Let me finish. (To Carl.)* When things weren't going his way, he kidnapped my violin.
CARL. I know.
ELLIOT. *(To Alan.)* He broke your bow, for god's sake!
DORIAN. Not his good bow.
ELLIOT. *(To Dorian.)* We nearly fell apart because of you. Would have, if I hadn't fired you first.
CARL. I'm no longer sure that Dorian was the problem. At least, not the only one.
ELLIOT. *How can you say that?*
CARL. This week there have been tantrums, too, and obstinacy.
ELLIOT. That's / because —
CARL. Granted, no bows were broken …
ELLIOT. If these two hadn't been sniffing each other —
ALAN. Hey / now.
GRACE. That's not true.
CARL. Bottom line, *his* stubbornness made the music better. Always. *(Beat.)*
ELLIOT. I can't believe I'm hearing this …
CARL. *(To Alan.)* And if he's found a physician who can … regulate him, then I think we should consider his proposal.
ELLIOT. Alan, you can't agree with him,
ALAN. El, it's not like —
ELLIOT. You can't, you can't let him / twist this —
CARL. *Let him talk. (Beat.)*
ALAN. I think there's some truth in it;
ELLIOT. *No!*
ALAN. I'm sorry, but there is. *(Beat.)*
DORIAN. *(Looking at Grace.)* When I heard her in Pittsburgh, I started to imagine a sound, a vibrant, muscular sound — not a *blend,* not a four-way compromise, but something greater than the sum of its parts. *(To Alan.)* It's a wonderful sound; I can hear it.
ELLIOT. Because you're *delusional.*
DORIAN. No, it's possible. Carl knows it's possible, don't you. *(Beat. Carl nods.)* Alan?
ALAN. I don't know.
DORIAN. Tell the truth.
ALAN. Maybe. Probably.
ELLIOT. How can you say that?

ALAN. *He plays better than you!* He hears things we don't hear. That's why we always put up with it when he got … *(He searches for the word.)*
DORIAN. Buggy.
ALAN. *Unpredictable.* Now you're unpredictable. But it doesn't seem worth putting up with. You're just not good enough to be unpredictable. *(Beat.)* I hate to say it, but it's true. *(Pause.)*
CARL. Is that your vote, then?
ALAN. I wasn't voting, I / was just —
CARL. Then vote.
ALAN. Do we have to do this here?
CARL. I didn't want to, but now we've started, so we're going to finish it. Are you in? *(Pause.)*
ALAN. Yeah, I guess.
CARL. Fine. Then it comes down to Grace.
GRACE. Me?
CARL. Would you be willing to stay? As far as I'm concerned, if you take the orchestra gig, we're through.
ALAN. Not necessarily.
CARL. Well, I'm through. I don't want to play with Richard, or Manzer, or the guy with the hair. We're not a machine. You can't just pop out a gear and plug in another. *(Beat. Alan turns to Grace.)*
ALAN. Well? What do you think? *(Beat.)*
ELLIOT. *(To Carl.)* Were you planning to tell her what the doctor said? *(Grace looks at Elliot.)* I'd think she deserves to know.
GRACE. *(To Carl.)* Doctor?
ELLIOT. *(To Grace.)* Entomologist. *(To Carl.)* After all, she's weighing job offers.
ALAN. You little shit.
GRACE. *(Half to herself.)* Oh my God …
ALAN. Goddamnit, El …
ELLIOT. *(To Alan.)* She's got her future to think of!
GRACE. You're sick? *(Carl nods.)*
ELLIOT. *(To Carl.)* When will the treatments start?
DORIAN. Don't do this, Nelly.
ELLIOT. Last time you were out of commission / for —
ALAN. Will you shut up!
CARL. *(To Grace.)* I'm sorry, I should've —
ALAN. *Don't apologize.*
CARL. *(Pointedly.)* I wasn't sure you needed to know. *(Beat.)*

ELLIOT. Well. Now she knows. And can make an informed decision. *(Pause.)*
GRACE. Can I have a few days to —
CARL. No.
ALAN. Carl …
CARL. I want it decided now.
ALAN. For God's sake, at least / give her —
CARL. *And I don't have time to argue about it. (To Grace.)* If you want to stay, then stay, if not, we'll split up. *(Everyone looks to Grace. She looks at Elliot, then Alan, then Dorian. Finally, to Carl:)*
GRACE. I'll stay.
CARL. With Dorian taking Elliot's place.
GRACE. Yes. *(Pause. Elliot is dazed.)*
CARL. All right, then. That's settled. *(Carl turns to Elliot.)*
ELLIOT. *(Quietly.)* You're making a huge / mistake. All of you.
CARL. "Please be advised that your employment with the Lazara Quartet is / hereby terminated."
ELLIOT. Mark my words, you won't last a month!
ALAN. Sorry, El. I wish it could have worked out otherwise.
CARL. We'll send you a check for tonight. *(Beat. Elliot goes to his violin case and begins to pack up. Dorian moves toward him.)*
DORIAN. Aren't you forgetting something?
ELLIOT. If you're all expecting a farewell hug, I'm afraid you're going to be disappointed.
GRACE. I think he's referring to the violin. *(Beat.)*
DORIAN. Hand it over, Nelly.
ELLIOT. It's mine. *(He backs up, holding the violin.)*
ALAN. It belongs to the quartet.
ELLIOT. Nobody's played it but me since we started.
GRACE. It's not yours.
ALAN. *(Moving towards Elliot.)* Don't make this harder than it needs to be.
ELLIOT. No, you can't have it. *(He clutches the violin to his chest.)*
ALAN. Carl?
DORIAN. Give it to me. *(He grabs the violin.)*
ELLIOT. Let go!
DORIAN. Alan? *(Alan moves in to help wrest the violin away from Elliot.)*
CARL. Knock it off, now.
DORIAN. *(To Elliot.)* Don't be a prick about it, / Nelly.

ALAN. Give it to him.
DORIAN. Let go.
CARL. Stop it.
GRACE. Just hand it over.
ELLIOT. No!
CARL. *I said stop it!* This isn't a rec room. *(Dorian and Alan release their grips. To Elliot:)* Let me have it.
ELLIOT. No!
CARL. Just for now.
ELLIOT. You'll give it to him.
CARL. I won't.
ELLIOT. You will.
CARL. I promise. No one else will play it.
ALAN. Carl, it be/longs —
CARL. *Quiet. (Pause. Carl takes hold of the violin. To Elliot.)* Trust me. I'm not going to give it to Dorian. *(Pause. Elliot relinquishes it.)*
DORIAN. *(To Carl.)* You took the viola from me, it's only fair / that —
CARL. *(Barely holding it together.)* This is beneath us, this … petty … Especially tonight. After playing that music? And thinking of all we sacrificed, all of us, for years. To wind up fighting over a fucking piece of *wood?*
ALAN. It's more than / just —
CARL. No, I'm sorry, that's not why I do this. *(He gr[illegible] the violin by the neck.)*
ELLIOT. What are you — *(Carl raises it over his head. Grace gasps.)*
ALAN. Carl, / no!
DORIAN. Don't! *(Carl smashes the back of the violin against the top of the chair back. The instrument explodes. Elliot lets out a cry, as if struck himself. Carl strikes it again, if necessary, insuring that it has splintered.)*
GRACE. Oh my god … *(Grace turns away, grabbing onto Alan's arm. Carl is visibly shaken; the others are in shock. Lights begin to shift.)*
ALAN. Jesus, Carl.
CARL. I didn't want it to come to this …
ELLIOT. Oh, god … *(Elliot grabs onto the chair and drops to his knees.)*
CARL. Never. But we were starting to lose perspective. *(He drops the neck and scroll of the violin. Still struggling to hold it together:)*

Now, we've got some repertoire to learn, so we'll have to make good use of time. *(Elliot reaches down to pick up shards of the violin from the floor.)* I may only be able to rehearse a few days a month. *(Dorian places his hand on Elliot's shoulder.) Does everybody understand? (He looks around at the others.)* We haven't got time to waste. *(Lights fade.)*

Scene 16

Music: the "Adagio" from Beethoven's String Quartet in F-Major, Opus 59, Number 1. [CD track #31.] Pin spot rises on Alan, in interview mode.

ALAN. *End? (He chuckles.)* Why should it end? I mean … Our recording of the Bartóks just won a Grammy! We're booked for the next two years. By the time this documentary's done, our Beethoven cycle will be in the can. So, end, no, I don't see why it should ever — Well, obviously it's got to end *sometime,* right? I mean, we're not *immortal,* we're all gonna — *(Beat.)* Which, actually, when you think about it, would — *(Beat.)* Huh. *(He smiles, thinks about it for a moment, then elaborates:)* Maybe that's how it should happen — you know, Elliot, Dorian, Carl and me, all of us in our *nineties,* white-haired, missing teeth, playing the "Adagio" from Opus Fifty-nine, Number One. In the *Concertgebouw.* And we come to a rest in the middle of the movement and stop, just … stop. *(The music stops.)* At the exact same moment. And the sound dies. And so do we. Right there, in the space of that rest, in unison. Like a single instrument.

And that's it. The rest is silence. *(Beat.)* Didn't somebody say that? "The rest is silence"?

You play your part the best you can till you run out of notes, and the rest … is … *(He gestures into the void. Lights fade. In darkness, the fugue finale of Beethoven's Opus 59, Number 3. [CD track #32.])*

End of Play

PROPERTY LIST

String instruments
Clip microphones
Music stands, sheet music
Sheet of paper
Folded piece of paper
Cell phone
Small envelope with engraved invitation
2 cups of coffee
Money
Cup of tea
Cloth
Sandwich
Stuffed animal or riding toy
Nickel
Pacifier
Boom box
Toilet plunger
Ransom note
Key
Handkerchief
Mug of hot water
Mug of hot water with presidential seal
Crossword puzzle, pen
Piece of cheesecake
Invitation

SOUND EFFECTS

(not included on music CD)

Sounds of a string quartet tuning
Doorbell buzzer
Teakettle whistle
Bach concerto for two violins, third movement ("Allegro")
1960's California–sound ballad
Pans clattering
Cabinets shutting
Applause